Master the Raspberry Pi Pico in C: WiFi with lwIP & mbedtls

**Harry Fairhead
&
Mike James**

**I/O Press
I Programmer Library**

Harry Fairhead & Mike James,
Master the Raspberry Pi Pico in C: WiFi with lwIP & mbedtls
ISBN Paperback: 9781871962819
ISBN Hardback: 9781871962079
First Printing, 2023
Revision 0

Published by IO Press   www.iopress.info
In association with I Programmer   www.i-programmer.info
and with I o T Programmer   www.iot-programmer.com

The publisher recognizes and respects all marks used by companies and manufacturers as a means to distinguish their products. All brand names and product names mentioned in this book are trade marks or service marks of their respective companies and our omission of trade marks is not an attempt to infringe on the property of others.

In particular we acknowledge that Raspberry Pi and Pico are registered trademarks of the Raspberry Pi Foundation.

For updates, errata, links to resources and the source code for the programs in this book, visit its dedicated page on the IO Press website: www.iopress.info.

Preface

The Raspberry Pi Pico W adds WiFi to the standard Pico and this makes it a true IoT device because it can connect with the Internet. You can think of the Pico W as a superset of the original – everything you can do with an original Pico you can do with a Pico W, but not vice versa. The extra capabilities added to the Pico W open up lots of possibilities, but only if you are prepared to do battle with the two libraries that provide networking and security – lwIP and mbedtls respectively. The problem with these large libraries of code is that, particularly in the case of mbedtls, they are poorly documented. What documentation you can find generally doesn't refer directly to the Pico W and its SDK and can be difficult to follow.

The purpose of this book is to provide a guide to using both of these libraries. It can't be complete because they are large and the range of things you might want to do with them is huge. This book mostly covers protocols based on TCP/IP, but UDP is also used where appropriate. We cover making basic network connections and then tackle the basics of implementing an HTTP client. As well as covering the basic mechanics of using lwIP, we also concentrate on how to organize the use of an asynchronous library based on callbacks. This is mostly a matter of introducing a state variable which can be used to control the main polling loop. This is a much better approach for IoT applications than trying to organize a sequence of callbacks to implement the essentially linear logic of connect, send, receive, process, etc. Although the use of the lwIP and mbedtls libraries is explained with reference to the Pico SDK, the same principles will apply to any hardware that makes use of the libraries without an operating system.

A particular problem with IoT networking is the apparent need for the IoT device to behave as a server to allow it to send data to other devices. It isn't as well known as it should be that, even in the role of a client, a device can send data to a server and so avoid the overhead of being a server itself.

The problem of IoT security is unique because IoT devices can be physically accessed by an attacker and hence any secrets embedded in their code have to be considered almost as public knowledge. Even so it is worth implementing encryption and this is achieved using mbedtls to create an HTTPS client. The advantage of this is that the client can use encryption without having to store a certificate and hence a private key.

If you can ensure the physical security of the IoT device, then running it as a server is possible and this is covered in both HTTP and HTTPS modes, complete with certificates. The mbedtls library supports lots of different security features and we cover the basics of cryptography, including the problem of generating random numbers, what an encryption suite is and the various modes of AES encryption. This should help you construct sensible and efficient configurations for mbedtls.

The later chapters are devoted to specific protocols, making use of both lwIP and mbedtls. We look at UDP as an alternative to implementing a server; SNTP as a way of setting the Pico W's real time clock; SMTP to allow email notifications and MQTT as a way of avoiding implementing a server and as a scalable architecture. Each of the chapters includes example programs which do the basics of the task.

None of the programs in this book are production level, as the object of the exercise is to show how things work. Our examples are as simple as they can possibly be and they lack error handling to make sure that you can see clearly how they work. By the same token this is not a projects book, but you can easily develop any of the examples into something more complete and incorporate them into your own projects, and the code is downloadable from the book's web page.

There are many topics that we haven't covered simply because there are so many possibles. One such "missing" topic is the use of the Pico W with Bluetooth. This is such a huge subject that it would need a book in its own right – feel free to contact us if you think such a book would be worthwhile. We also focus on using lwIP and mbedtls without an operating system, i.e. without RTOS. This restricts our attention to lwIP's raw module rather than the sockets module. While sockets are the way that non-IoT devices most often approach networking, the raw module is ideally suited to smaller devices and it avoids the problem of installing and getting to know RTOS.

We have settled on VS Code as our preferred IDE and it is a good choice for the Pico SDK. The details of setting up a development environment, summarized in Appendix A, are covered extensively in *Programming The Raspberry Pi Pico/W in C, 2nd Ed*, ISBN: 9781871962796, which is also where we cover the basics of sensors, PWM, I2C, GPIO, etc..

Thanks to our tireless editors Sue Gee and Kay Ewbank. who attempt to eliminate our mistakes and turn garbled text into smooth sentences. Doubtless errors remain, and we hope they are few.

For the source code for the programs in this book, together with any updates or errata and links to resources including recommendations for obtaining electronic components, visit its dedicated page on the IO Press website: iopress.info. You can also contact us at harry.fairhead@i-programmer.info or mike.james@i-programmer.info.

Harry Fairhead
Mike James
March, 2023

Table of Contents

Chapter 4
SSL/TLS and HTTPS   **81**

Chapter 5
Details of Cryptography   **97**

Chapter 9
SMTP For Email

187

Chapter 10
MQTT For The IoT

197

Appendix 1
Getting Started In C

209

Chapter 1

The Pico WiFi Stack

The Pico W has WiFi but it doesn't have an operating system. More specifically, it doesn't have the networking features of an operating system like Linux. As a result we have to rely on libraries to provide the same features. In the case of the Pico SDK we have the WiFi driver `cyw43_driver`, the `pico_cyw43_arch`, `pico_lwip` and `pico_mbedtls` libraries. These are all low level and present difficulties even if you are familiar with networking APIs such as sockets. This book is designed to make up for the lack of clear documentation and simple examples. The intention is not only to make sure that you can create something like a TCP client, but also that you know how it works.

Most of this book is about lwIP, lightweight IP, a library that provides much of the protocol support you would find in operating systems such as Linux. The second library that features extensively is mbedtls which can be used to provide security in the form of encryption. It is not so long ago that devices like the Pico were too small to engage in encrypted communication – today it is almost essential. Even so, the security of remote devices connected over the Internet (IoT devices) isn't the same as the considerations that apply to desktop machines. The final component in the mix is the support for Bluetooth in SDK 1.5. If you are using an earlier version you need to upgrade if you want to use mbedtls or Bluetooth.

It is assumed that you already know how to create, build and run programs for the Pico in C. If not the subject is covered in detail in *Programming The Raspberry Pi Pico/W in C, 2nd Ed*, ISBN: 9781871962796. The examples in this book have all been created using VS Code, but you can use any development system. The code for all of the examples can be found on the book's website at www.iopress.info. Many of the examples are developed step by step, building to a finished version. If there have been many steps then the complete program is also presented. To avoid repetition, for examples that involve minor changes to previous programs, a new complete listing isn't given, but you can find a complete listing on the website.

Architecture of the WiFi Stack

The Pico W has two libraries to make it possible to work with its WiFi without having to work at the level of the basic hardware. You can think of these libraries as forming a set of three levels.

The lowest level is the `cyw43_driver` which provides an interface to the hardware via the SPI interface that connects the Pico to the cyw43 WiFi chip. In most cases you can ignore the functions in this module as most of the functionality they provide is available via `pico_cyw43_arch`.

The `pico_cyw43_arch` library provides higher-level functions, mostly concerned with setting up the WiFi and making connections. This is documented and is a good place to start.

The `pico_lwip` is a set of wrapper functions around the lwIP open source IP stack. This has been ported to the Pico and works with IP, Internet Protocol, via the WiFi drivers. There is almost no documentation of `pico_lwip` but the original lwIP project is fully, if not particularly clearly, documented. It provides higher-level protocols based on IP (Internet Protocol) such as TCP (Transmission Control Protocol), UDP (User Datagram Protocol), DNS (Domain Name System or Service) and so on. After you have made the connect to a WiFi network it is `pico_lwip` that you use to do most of the work.

The CYW43439 Driver

The Pico W uses an Infineon CYW43439 which has a pair of ARM processors and is connected to the Pico via a simple 3-wire SPI bus. You can see the configuration from the official schematics:

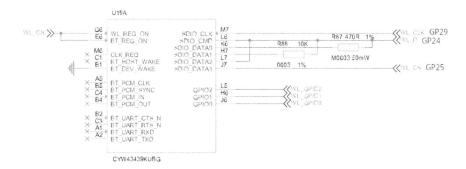

The CYW43439 has a 4-bit Secure Digital Input Output bus which originated with SD cards. The SDIO bus is an extension of the SPI protocol to use additional data lines. Typically a Quad or 4-bit mode is used with SD cards, usually called QSPI Quad SPI, but there are also 2-bit and 1-bit modes and a 2-line SPI mode. These modes are not true SPI as the data lines are bidirectional. The CYW43439 does support a true SPI interface, but the mode used with the Pico is SD 1-bit, which uses a single bidirectional data line.

The driver, which is stored in `pico-sdk/lib/cyw43-driver/` has two binary files which contain the program that is downloaded into the CYW43439. It also contains the C code for reading and writing data to the SPI bus and to particular registers.

To avoid having to use GPIO lines in SPI mode, the driver makes use of one of the PIOs. This means that you should avoid using the same PIO as the WiFi driver for general purpose I/O. Which PIO is used is set by:

```
#define CYW43_SPI_PIO_PREFERRED_PIO 1
```

You can override this if you want to, but it is simpler to use PIO 0 for your own PIO programs. The driver uses a single state machine and ten bytes of instruction memory. If you want to use PIO 1 in the unused memory you can use `pio_claim_unused_sm` to find a free state machine.

The cyw43_ll Module

The driver has a lower-level module `cyw43_ll` which deals directly with the hardware. You can find out more by reading:

```
pico-sdk/lib/cyw43-driver/src/cyw43_ll.h
pico-sdk/lib/cyw43-driver/src/cyw43_ll.c
```

Many of the functions are documented, but they are difficult to use unless you want to take over the complete running of the WiFi stack due to the difficulty of finding existing configuration parameters.

The driver has a number of functions that you can use, but in the main they are used by the higher-level software. The main reason for describing them here is to make it possible to debug low-level problems.

Most of these use the driver state `self` as a pointer to a `cyw43_t` struct. If you allow the driver to perform initialization then you can find this in the variable `cyw43_state` defined in:

```
pico-sdk/lib/cyw43-driver/src/cyw43_ctrl.c
```

That is, you can use `cyw43_state` wherever you see `self` in the function definitions. Similarly you can use `CYW43_ITF_STA` or `CYW43_ITF_AP` wherever you see `itf` as a parameter for client or access point mode.

Initialization and Connection

- `void cyw43_init(*self)`
  initializes the driver
- `void cyw43_deinit(*self)`
  shuts the driver down
- `void cyw43_wifi_set_up(*self, itf, up, country)`
  sets up and initializes WiFi where the up parameter is a boolean that controls access point mode
- `int cyw43_wifi_join(*self, ssid_len, *ssid, key_len, *key, auth_type, *bssid, channel)`
  connects or joins a WiFi network in Station mode (STA) with its Service Set IDentifier SSID `ssid`, using `key` and `auth_type`, which can be any of:
  - `CYW43_AUTH_OPEN`
  - `CYW43_AUTH_WPA_TKIP_PSK`
  - `CYW43_AUTH_WPA2_AES_PSK`
  - `CYW43_AUTH_WPA2_MIXED_PSK`

  `bssid` is either `NULL` or the MAC address of the access point and `channel` is the band to connect with if `bssid` is specified
- `int cyw43_wifi_leave(*self, itf)`
  disassociates from a WiFi network
- `void cyw43_cb_tcpip_init(*self, itf)`
  initializes the IP stack
- `void cyw43_cb_tcpip_deinit(*self, itf)`
  deinitializes the IP stack
- `Void cyw43_cb_tcpip_set_link_up(*self, itf)`
  notifies the IP stack that the link is up
- `void cyw43_cb_tcpip_set_link_down(*self, itf)`
  notifies the IP stack that the link is down

State

- `bool cyw43_is_initialized (*self)`
  determines if the cyw43 driver has been initialized
- `int cyw43_wifi_link_status (*self, itf)`
  gets the WiFi link status, which can be:
  - `CYW43_LINK_DOWN`   WiFi down
  - `CYW43_LINK_JOIN`   connected to WiFi
  - `CYW43_LINK_FAIL`   connection failed

- ◆ `CYW43_LINK_NONET`   no matching SSID found (could be out of range, or down)
- ◆ `CYW43_LINK_BADAUTH` authentication failure
- ◆ `int cyw43_tcpip_link_status (*self, itf)`
  gets the link status, which can be one of the previous five items plus:
  - ◆ `CYW43_LINK_NOIP` connected to WiFi without an IP address
  - ◆ `CYW43_LINK_UP`   connected to WiFi with an IP address
- ◆ `int cyw43_wifi_get_mac (*self, itf, mac[6])`
  gets the MAC address of the device as a 6-byte array
- ◆ `cyw43_wifi_get_rssi(*self, *rssi)`
  returns the signal strength of the current connection in `rssi`

Power Management

- ◆ `int cyw43_wifi_pm(*self, pm)`
  sets the WiFi power management mode according to `pm` an integer. The value of `pm` can be computed using a utility function.
- ◆ `uint32_t cyw43_pm_value(pm_mode, pm2_sleep_ret_ms, li_beacon_period, li_dtim_period, li_assoc)`
  where `pm_mode` is one of:
  - ◆ `CYW43_NO_POWERSAVE_MODE` no power saving
  - ◆ `CYW43_PM1_POWERSAVE_MODE` aggressive power saving which reduces WiFi throughput
  - ◆ `CYW43_PM2_POWERSAVE_MODE` power saving with high throughput (preferred), saves power when there is no WiFi activity for some time

  `pm2_sleep_ret_ms` maximum time to wait before going back to sleep for `CYW43_PM2_POWERSAVE_MODE` mode measured in milliseconds and must be between 10 and 2000ms and divisible by 10

  `li_beacon_period` wake interval measured in beacon periods

  `li_dtim_period` wake interval measured in DTIMs; if set to 0, the wake interval is measured in beacon periods

  `li_assoc` Wake interval sent to the access point

There are three predefined power saving settings:

- `CYW43_DEFAULT_PM` `cyw43_pm_value(`
  `CYW43_PM2_POWERSAVE_MODE, 200, 1, 1, 10)`

default power management mode

- `CYW43_AGGRESSIVE_PM` `cyw43_pm_value(`
  `CYW43_PM2_POWERSAVE_MODE, 2000, 1, 1, 10)`

aggressive power management mode for optimal power usage at the cost of performance

- `CYW43_PERFORMANCE_PM` `cyw43_pm_value(`
  `CYW43_PM2_POWERSAVE_MODE, 20, 1, 1, 1)`

performance power management mode where more power is used to increase performance

WiFi Scan

- `int cyw43_wifi_scan(*self, *opts, *env, result_cb)`
  performs a scan for WiFi networks

The `opts` parameter is currently ignored but must be set to `0`,

`env` is passed to the callback and `result_cb` is a callback for the scan results, called once for each access point found. It has the signature:

```
int scan_result(void *env, const
                        cyw43_ev_scan_result_t *result)
```

where the `result` parameter is a struct that gives the details of the access point:

`result.bssid`	access point MAC address in 6-byte array
`result.ssid_len`	length of WLAN access point name
`result.ssid_wlan`	access point name, max 32 bytes
`result.channel`	WiFi channel
`result.auth_mode`	WiFi auth mode
`rssi`	signal strength

- `bool cyw43_wifi_scan_active(*self)`
  determines if a WiFi scan is in progress

Access Point Mode

- `void cyw43_wifi_ap_set_ssid(*self, len, *buf)`
  sets the SSID for the access point
- `void cyw43_wifi_ap_get_ssid(*self, *len, **buf)`
  gets the SSID for the access point
- `void cyw43_wifi_ap_set_channel(*self, channel)`
  sets the channel for the access point
- `void cyw43_wifi_ap_set_password(*self, len, *buf)`
  sets the password for the WiFi access point

14

- void cyw43_wifi_ap_set_auth(*self, auth)
  sets the security authorization used in AP mode
- void cyw43_wifi_ap_get_max_stas (*self, *max_stas)
  gets the maximum number of devices (STAs) that can be associated
  with the wifi access point
- void cyw43_wifi_ap_get_stas(*self, *num_stas, *macs)
  gets the number of devices (STAs) associated with the WiFi access
  point

Miscellaneous

- int cyw43_ioctl(*self, cmd, len, *buf, itf)
  sends an I/O control command to CYW43

  cmd can be any of:
  - CYW43_IOCTL_GET_SSID
  - CYW43_IOCTL_GET_CHANNEL
  - CYW43_IOCTL_SET_DISASSOC
  - CYW43_IOCTL_GET_ANTDIV
  - CYW43_IOCTL_SET_ANTDIV   set to 0 for on-chip antenna
  - CYW43_IOCTL_SET_MONITOR   not implemented
  - CYW43_IOCTL_GET_RSSI
  - CYW43_IOCTL_GET_VAR
  - CYW43_IOCTL_SET_VAR

- int cyw43_send_ethernet(*self, itf, len, *buf, is_pbuf)
  Send a raw Ethernet packet. The buf which can be a byte buffer or a
  PBUF contains the MAC address of the destination. You don't need a
  receive ethernet function because this is a raw IP packet as explained
  in Chapter 2.

Driver and lwIP Operating Modes

WiFi hardware needs periodic attention and when used with an operating
system this is usually taken care of by multithreading, but the Pico doesn't
have an operating system unless you install one and for most applications
this isn't a good idea. While you can install and use RTOS (Real Time
Operating System) this would take us into a whole new area and style of
program development. Using RTOS just to run WiFi is not a good choice, but
using RTOS to schedule tasks means that managing the WiFi can be one of
them. This book doesn't cover using RTOS to manage WiFi.

The pico_cyw43_arch library provides three different ways of achieving the
regular attention that the hardware needs. The first relies on polling, the
second uses interrupts and the third makes use of the "threads" provided by
the FreeRTOS operating system.

The mode used depends on which library you link to in `CmakeLists.txt`.

The first is `pico_cyw43_arch_lwip_poll`. Using this library the client program has to call `cyw43_arch_poll()` every so often to allow it to run the WiFi software so that it can call callbacks and generally move data. You can also use `cyw43_arch_wait_for_work_until()` to wait until the WiFi needs attention, at which point you can call `cyw43_arch_poll()` to service it.

This is a very simple arrangement as it is entirely synchronous and there is no danger of a race condition and hence no need for locking of any kind. It has the disadvantage that it is not multi-core nor interrupt-safe. That is, if you are running code on the second core, or if you are making use of interrupts, the networking code can be interrupted in ways that corrupt the data. Notice that polling makes use of an interrupt on GPIO 24 to signal that the WiFi hardware needs attention, but the service routine doesn't interact with the user application and so it is safe.

The second choice is `pico_cyw43_arch_lwip_threadsafe_background`. In this case there is nothing the client program has to do and the driver and lwIP code is called by an interrupt. This is multi-core and interrupt-safe, but only if you use locking when you call lwIP code. All callbacks are called in interrupt mode. Any code not run by lwIP has to be bracketed by the instructions `cyw43_arch_lwip_begin` and `cyw43_arch_lwip_end`. These apply locks which stop interrupts and other cores running the code at the same time. You don't have to bracket calls to lwIP made within callbacks because these are being run by lwIP, but if you do they have no effect.

The final choice is `pico_cyw43_arch_lwip_sys_freertos`. The freeRTOS operating system adds the ability to run multiple tasks at different levels of priority – it provides a basic "threads" capability. This allows the lwIP software to run independently and in an organized way with your custom code. The installation and use of freeRTOS is a big undertaking and entails a complete change in the way that you schedule tasks. As already stated, in most cases it is best avoided for simple WiFi applications.

In the rest of this book the examples will use the `threadsafe_background` mode, but it is easy to convert them to polling mode by adding calls to `cyw43_arch_poll()`.

It is important to notice that you can only use lwIP sockets if you are also using freeRTOS. Without freeRTOS you are limited to the "raw" lwIP APIs. It is also worth mentioning that there is a non-WiFi mode, set by using `pico_cyw43_arch_none`, which disables WiFi but allows access to the onboard LED.

Using threadsafe_background

The `threadsafe_background` mode of operation makes use of a timer interrupt to regularly run the WiFi driver and lwIP code and a GPIO interrupt to signal that the WiFi hardware needs attention.

SDK 1.5 introduced async context which replaces the ad-hoc system of locks used previously. An async context doesn't call any functions concurrently and it runs on a single core – it is a single thread of execution on a specific core. It can have multiple functions registered and these can be interrupt or timer driven. They are all run on the same core and only one can be executing at any given moment.

A standard alarm timer is used and the interrupt interval is set to 50 ms which gives you a rough idea of how often you need to call `cyw43_arch_poll()` if you do opt for polling mode. The interrupt interval is set by `CYW43_SLEEP_CHECK_MS`.

As already mentioned, the WiFi hardware uses a GPIO interrupt on GP24 within the same async context to signal that there is data that needs servicing.

All of these workers operate within the same async context and so they do not interfere with each other's operation, but of course your app doesn't and it needs to interact with the WiFi and lwIP. The solution is for your app to acquire a lock on the async context before making use of the driver or the lwIP library. Before release 1.5 a lock was achieved in a more ad-hoc way and you needed to call:

`cyw43_arch_lwip_begin();`

and

`cyw43_arch_lwip_end();`

to acquire and release the lock. These can still be used, but they are converted into:

`async_context_acquire_lock_blocking(cyw43_async_context);`

and

`async_context_release_lock(cyw43_async_context);`

You can use either method of locking the driver and lwIP library code before you make use of it. Notice that you only have to lock when there is a chance that your use of a driver or lwIP function could be interrupted by another driver or lwIP function that uses the same shared resources.

cyw43_arch Functions

There is a small list of well-documented functions in the `cyw43_arch` library. They are all concerned with configuring the WiFi and not with transferring data.

The first group of functions are concerned with initialization:

- `int cyw43_arch_init(void)`
  initializes the hardware to the default country
- `int cyw43_arch_init_with_country(uint32_t country)`
  initializes the hardware to the specific country
- `uint32_t cyw43_arch_get_country_code(void)`
  returns the country code of the current setup of the WiFi
- `void cyw43_arch_deinit(void)`
  deinitializes the hardware and the software

The initialization also calls `lwip_init()` to prepare the lwIP library for use. You don't need to explicitly call this as the lwIP documentation suggests.

The country code sets the range of frequencies that can be used. If you don't specify a code then the WiFi hardware is configured to use only the channels allowed in every country. The country codes are listed in the `cyw43_driver` documentation.

There are two functions which select the WiFi as a client, `sta`, or an access point, `ap`:

- `void cyw43_arch_enable_sta_mode(void)`
- `void cyw43_arch_enable_ap_mode(const char *ssid,`
  `const char *password, uint32_t auth)`

There are three functions that, after the hardware has been initialized, make a connection to an access point:

- `int cyw43_arch_wifi_connect_blocking(const char *ssid,`
  `const char *pw, uint32_t auth)`
- `int cyw43_arch_wifi_connect_bssid_blocking(const char *ssid,`
  `const uint8_t *bssid, const char *pw, uint32_t auth)`
- `int cyw43_arch_wifi_connect_timeout_ms(const char *ssid,`
  `const char *pw, uint32_t auth, uint32_t timeout)`
- `int cyw43_arch_wifi_connect_bssid_timeout_ms(const char`
  `id, const uint8_t *bssid, const char *pw,`
  `uint32_t auth, uint32_t timeout_ms)`
- `int cyw43_arch_wifi_connect_async(const char *ssid,`
  `const char *pw, uint32_t auth)`
- `int cyw43_arch_wifi_connect_bssid_async(const char *ssid,`
  `const uint8_t *bssid, const char *pw, uint32_t auth)`

Notice that there are three types of connect – blocking, timeout and async and each has an ssid only and ssid plus bssid version. The ssid is the name of the access point and the bssid is its MAC address. You can specify the MAC address as a security measure as ssids are easy to spoof but a MAC address is supposed to be unique.

The auth parameter sets the type of authorization supported.

In most cases WPA2_MIXED is the best choice.

Finally there are two functions which provide access to the GPIO lines that the WiFi hardware supports:

- void cyw43_arch_gpio_put (uint wl_gpio, bool value)
- bool cyw43_arch_gpio_get (uint wl_gpio)

These functions provide enough to make a connection to an access point.

Connecting To WiFi

Connecting the Pico to a WiFi Access Point (AP) is the "Hello World" of WiFi programming and it is generally the best place to start. If you cannot make a connection to an AP then you cannot move on to more interesting things.

It is assumed that you have a serial connection to the Pico W and can see output sent to it by printf. The reason is that the software sends connection status messages via the serial link and this allows you to track progress and see if there are any problems. You can stop the status information being sent to the serial port by setting the build to Release.

The first thing to do is initialize the hardware and the libraries:

```
if (cyw43_arch_init_with_country(CYW43_COUNTRY_mylocation))
{
    printf("failed to initialize\n");
    return 1;
}
```

This also sets the country code so that the hardware knows what channels and power it can use. Alternatively you can use cyw43_arch_init which uses the country set by PICO_CYW43_ARCH_DEFAULT_COUNTRY_CODE in cyw43_arch.h.

Once the system is initialized you can attempt a connection:

```
cyw43_arch_enable_sta_mode();
if (cyw43_arch_wifi_connect_blocking(ssid, pass,
                            CYW43_AUTH_WPA2_MIXED_PSK))
    {
        printf("failed to connect\n");
        return 1;
    }
```

First we have to set the WiFi into client mode and then we attempt the connection. You have to supply the SSID and password to connect and connection can take a few seconds. While the connection is being made you will see messages via the serial connection:

```
cyw43 loaded ok, mac 28:cd:c1:00:56:34
API: 12.2
Data: RaspberryPi.PicoW
Compiler: 1.29.4
ClmImport: 1.47.1
Customization: v5 22/06/24
Creation: 2022-06-24 06:55:08
connect status: joining
connect status: no ip
connect status: link up
```

The time between the no ip message and link up can be quite long depending on how long the DHCP server takes to allocate an IP address. When you see link up the connection has been made and the client has an IP address ready to communicate.

This is all so standard we might as well put it together into a function and add a main program to use it:

```
#include <stdio.h>
#include "pico/stdlib.h"
#include "pico/cyw43_arch.h"


int setup(uint32_t country, const char *ssid, const char *pass,
                                             uint32_t auth)
{

   if (cyw43_arch_init_with_country(country))
   {
     return 1;
   }
   cyw43_arch_enable_sta_mode();
   if (cyw43_arch_wifi_connect_blocking(ssid, pass, auth))
   {
     return 2;
   }
}
```

```c
char ssid[] = "myhost";
char pass[] = "mypassword";
uint32_t country = CYW43_COUNTRY_mycountry;
uint32_t auth = CYW43_AUTH_WPA2_MIXED_PSK;

int main()
{
    stdio_init_all();
    setup(country, ssid, pass, auth);
    while (true)
    {
        sleep_ms(1);
    }
}
```

The setup function makes the connection to the WiFi AP that you have specified the SSID and password for. The while loop just keeps the main program active while all this goes on.

To run this program you need a CmakeLists.txt and it has some additional instructions:

```
cmake_minimum_required(VERSION 3.13)
set(PICO_BOARD pico_w)
set(CMAKE_C_STANDARD 11)
set(CMAKE_CXX_STANDARD 17)

include(pico_sdk_import.cmake)
project(PicoW C CXX ASM)
pico_sdk_init()

add_executable(main
 main.c
)

target_include_directories(main PRIVATE ${CMAKE_CURRENT_LIST_DIR})
target_link_libraries(main pico_stdlib
                      pico_cyw43_arch_lwip_threadsafe_background)
pico_add_extra_outputs(main)
```

Here the program is stored in main.c. Notice that you need the set(PICO_BOARD pico_w) instruction to compile the program. The use of the pico_cyw43_arch_lwip_threadsafe_background library means that we don't have to poll. If you select the pico_cyw43_arch_lwip_poll instead everything works the same, but you have to include a call to cyw43_arch_poll() in the final while loop.

We also need to copy pico_sdk_import.cmake into the root of the project. You can get it from any existing project, but you can get an up-to-date copy from pico/pico-sdk/external. In addition we need a copy of a WiFi header file, lwipopts_examples_common.h, from the pico-examples/pico_w folder, which needs renaming to `lwipopts.h`. The `lwipopts.h` file sets the defaults for the operation of the lwIP library. You can make your own, but the example file is a good starting point.

Once you have assembled all this, you can compile and run the program. You should see it go through the various stages of connecting to the WiFi AP. If you don't then check the SSID, password and authentication method. Make sure that you can connect via a phone or other device using the same credentials.

A Connect Function

Virtually every program in this book starts by connecting to WiFi, so it makes sense to create a reasonably good connection function and keep it in its own C file with a suitable header. For simplicity, however, it is more direct to create a header file containing the function that can be used in all of the examples.

The `setup` function given in the previous section is good enough while you are debugging, but it would be even better to have visual feedback using the onboard LED. To do this we need to use the asynchronous version of the connection function and we need to check the status to modify the speed of flashing of the LED:

```
int setup(uint32_t country, const char *ssid, const char *pass,
                                                uint32_t auth)
{

    if (cyw43_arch_init_with_country(country))
    {
        return 1;
    }
    cyw43_arch_enable_sta_mode();

    if (cyw43_arch_wifi_connect_async(ssid, pass, auth))
    {
        return 2;
    }
    int flashrate = 1000;
    int status = CYW43_LINK_UP + 1;
    while (status >= 0 && status != CYW43_LINK_UP)
    {
        int new_status = cyw43_tcpip_link_status(&cyw43_state,
                                                CYW43_ITF_STA);
```

```
    if (new_status != status)
        {
            status = new_status;
            flashrate = flashrate / (status + 1);
            printf("connect status: %d %d\n", status, flashrate);
        }
        cyw43_arch_gpio_put(CYW43_WL_GPIO_LED_PIN, 1);
        sleep_ms(flashrate);
        cyw43_arch_gpio_put(CYW43_WL_GPIO_LED_PIN, 0);
        sleep_ms(flashrate);
    }
    if (status < 0)
    {
        cyw43_arch_gpio_put(CYW43_WL_GPIO_LED_PIN, 0);
    }
    else
    {
        cyw43_arch_gpio_put(CYW43_WL_GPIO_LED_PIN, 1);
    }
    return status;
}
```

If you use this extended setup function the onboard LED starts to flash slowly and speeds up with each stage of connection. If the function ends without an error, the LED is left on, otherwise it is turned off. You can modify the function to give more information by using different flash rates.

If you are puzzled by the way the status is handled, the reason for the initial int status = CYW43_LINK_UP + 1 is that the status isn't updated until the first change of status and so you have to initialize it to a value that cannot be returned as a valid status code. After this you can detect changes in the status and react accordingly.

lwIP NETIF

Once the WiFi connection has been made, most of the details of the IP connection are handled by lwIP. There is some duplication in function in the cyw43_arch module, but there is an argument that you should prefer lwIP as this is machine-independent.

Among the modules in the lwIP library it is the NETIF module that provides access to the raw network interface. The WiFi driver provides the connection but it is the NETIF module that supplies the IP setup – IP address, netmask, gateway, host name, etc.

As an example of making use of it we can add some calls to the setup function to discover the IP address that has been assigned. When the WiFi connection is set up, a struct, `netif_default`, is created which contains the details of the default connection. Three fields give the details of the IP connection:

- ◆ `ip_addr_t ip_addr; //IP address`
- ◆ `ip_addr_t netmask; //Subnet mask`
- ◆ `ip_addr_t gw;      //Gateway address`

You can use these directly and there are macros which convert the raw address into alternative formats. For example:

```
printf("IP: %s\n", ip4addr_ntoa( &(netif_default->ip_addr)));
printf("Mask: %s\n", ip4addr_ntoa(&(netif_default->netmask)));
printf("Gateway: %s\n", ip4addr_ntoa(&(netif_default->gw)));
```

displays:

```
IP: 192.168.253.46
Mask: 255.255.255.0
Gateway: 192.168.253.1
```

There are also access macros which can be used to simplify access to the `struct` and protect it from any changes to its implementation:

```
printf("IP: %s\n", ip4addr_ntoa(netif_ip_addr4(netif_default)));
printf("Mask: %s\n",
                    ip4addr_ntoa(netif_ip_netmask4(netif_default)));
printf("Gateway: %s\n", ip4addr_ntoa(netif_ip_gw4(netif_default)));
```

You can also get the current host name, by default `PicoW`, using:

```
printf("Host Name: %s\n", netif_get_hostname(netif_default) );
```

Adding these four lines to the end of the setup function provides some additional information.

You can use `netif_set_hostname` to set the host name but you have to be careful to do it after setting client mode and before the connect:

```
cyw43_arch_enable_sta_mode();
netif_set_hostname(netif_default,"MyPicoW");
if (cyw43_arch_wifi_connect_async(ssid, pass, auth))
```

You can add an extra parameter to the setup function to set the host name.

The final common customization is to set a fixed IP address. To do this properly we should really turn off the DHCP client, but this seems to be difficult to do without modifying the SDK. The simplest solution is to allow any DHCP server to assign an IP address etc, and then modify them:

```
ip_addr_t ip;
IP4_ADDR(&ip, 192, 168, 253, 210);
netif_set_ipaddr(netif_default, &ip);
IP4_ADDR(&ip, 255, 255, 255, 0);
netif_set_netmask(netif_default, &ip);
IP4_ADDR(&ip, 192, 168, 253, 202);
netif_set_gw(netif_default, &ip);
```

These modifications have to be made after the WiFi connection is complete. Ideally the new IP address should be to a range that isn't controlled by DHCP. A better solution is to set the DHCP server to allocate a fixed address to the Pico.

A Connection Function

Putting all this together gives the complete setup function which should be stored in setupWifi.h:

```
int setup(uint32_t country, const char *ssid, const char *pass,
            uint32_t auth, const char *hostname, ip_addr_t *ip,
                                ip_addr_t *mask, ip_addr_t *gw)
{
    if (cyw43_arch_init_with_country(country))
    {
        return 1;
    }
    cyw43_arch_enable_sta_mode();
    if (hostname != NULL)
    {
        netif_set_hostname(netif_default, hostname);
    }
    if (cyw43_arch_wifi_connect_async(ssid, pass, auth))
    {
        return 2;
    }

    int flashrate = 1000;
    int status = CYW43_LINK_UP + 1;

    while (status >= 0 && status != CYW43_LINK_UP)
    {
        int new_status = cyw43_tcpip_link_status(&cyw43_state,
                                        CYW43_ITF_STA);
```

```c
        if (new_status != status)
        {
            status = new_status;
            flashrate = flashrate / (status + 1);
            printf("connect status: %d %d\n", status, flashrate);
        }
        cyw43_arch_gpio_put(CYW43_WL_GPIO_LED_PIN, 1);
        sleep_ms(flashrate);
        cyw43_arch_gpio_put(CYW43_WL_GPIO_LED_PIN, 0);
        sleep_ms(flashrate);
    }

    if (status < 0)
    {
        cyw43_arch_gpio_put(CYW43_WL_GPIO_LED_PIN, 0);
    }
    else
    {
        cyw43_arch_gpio_put(CYW43_WL_GPIO_LED_PIN, 1);
        if (ip != NULL)
        {
            netif_set_ipaddr(netif_default, ip);
        }
        if (mask != NULL)
        {
            netif_set_netmask(netif_default, mask);
        }
        if (gw != NULL)
        {
            netif_set_gw(netif_default, gw);
        }

        printf("IP: %s\n",
                ip4addr_ntoa(netif_ip_addr4(netif_default)));
        printf("Mask: %s\n",
                ip4addr_ntoa(netif_ip_netmask4(netif_default)));
        printf("Gateway: %s\n",
                ip4addr_ntoa(netif_ip_gw4(netif_default)));
        printf("Host Name: %s\n",
                netif_get_hostname(netif_default));
    }

    return status;
}
```

This function can now be used to specify IP address, mask and gateway:

```
ip_addr_t ip;
IP4_ADDR(&ip, 192, 168, 253, 210);
ip_addr_t mask;
IP4_ADDR(&mask, 255, 255, 255, 0);
ip_addr_t gw;
IP4_ADDR(&gw, 192, 168, 253, 202);

setup(country, ssid, pass, auth, "MyPicoW", &ip, &mask, &gw);
```

or simply accept the assigned values:

```
setup(country, ssid, pass, auth, "MyPicoW", NULL, NULL, NULL);
```

Notice that no locking is required as the calls to the driver and lwIP don't involve shared resources that could be corrupted by an interrupt.

It is also a time saver to include a connect function in the header file with details of your testing access point:

```
int connect()
{
    char ssid[] = "ssid";
    char pass[] = "password";
    uint32_t country = CYW43_COUNTRY_code;
    uint32_t auth = CYW43_AUTH_WPA2_MIXED_PSK;
    return  setup(country, ssid, pass, auth, "MyPicoW",
                                      NULL, NULL, NULL);
}
```

It is assumed that this header file is available for all of the examples that follow.

To make use of it with a main program you need a `CmakeLists.txt` file, also a copy of `pico_sdk_import.cmake` and we need a copy of a WiFi header file, `lwipopts_examples_common.h`, from the `pico-examples/pico_w` folder, which needs renaming to `lwipopts.h`.

Scan

As a second example of using the driver functions we can perform a scan to discover what access points are available. This makes use of the function:

```
int cyw43_wifi_scan(*self, *opts, *env, result_cb)
```

This is a driver function and nothing to do with lwIP. Currently `opts` has to be set to 0 and the `result_cb` is a callback that is passed each result of the scan in turn. Notice that each access point may be listed more than once and it is up to you to filter duplicates.

The call back receives a struct with the access point's details:

result.bssid[6];	access point MAC address
result.ssid_len;	length of WLAN access point name
result.ssid[32];	WLAN access point name
result.channel;	WiFi channel
result.auth_mode;	authorization mode
result.rssi;	signal strength

A program to make one scan and report the results is:

```
#include <stdio.h>
#include "pico/stdlib.h"
#include "pico/cyw43_arch.h"

static int scan_result(void *env,
                          const cyw43_ev_scan_result_t *result)
{
    if (result)
    {
        printf("ssid: %-32s rssi: %4d chan: %3d
            mac: %02x:%02x:%02x:%02x:%02x:%02x sec: %u\n",
             result->ssid, result->rssi, result->channel,
              result->bssid[0], result->bssid[1], result→bssid[2],
               result->bssid[3], result->bssid[4],
                 result->bssid[5],
                   result->auth_mode);
    }
    return 0;
}

int main()
{
    stdio_init_all();

    if (cyw43_arch_init())
    {
        printf("failed to initialise\n");
        return 1;
    }

    cyw43_arch_enable_sta_mode();
    cyw43_wifi_set_up(&cyw43_state, CYW43_ITF_STA,
                                    true, CYW43_COUNTRY_UK);
    cyw43_wifi_scan_options_t scan_options = {0};
    int err = cyw43_wifi_scan(&cyw43_state, &scan_options,
                                    NULL, scan_result);
```

```
    while (true)
    {
        if (!cyw43_wifi_scan_active(&cyw43_state))
            break;
        sleep_ms(1000);
        printf("Scan in progress \n");
    }
    printf("Scan Complete\n");
    cyw43_arch_deinit();
    return 0;
}
```

The CmakeLists.txt file is the same as before as is the lwipopts.h. If you run the program you will see lines like:

```
ssid: Galaxy M110750 rssi:-50 chan: 2 mac: d6:3a:94:8a:2f:11 sec: 5
```

Getting the Signal Strength

Sometimes you just want the signal strength of an access point given by the Received Signal Strength Indicator, RSSI. This is fairly easy to get using:

```
cyw43_wifi_get_rssi(*self, *rssi);
```

which returns the signal strength of the current connection in the rssi parameter. For example:

```
#include <stdio.h>
#include "pico/stdlib.h"
#include "pico/cyw43_arch.h"
#include "setupWifi.h"

int main()
{
    stdio_init_all();
    connect();
    int32_t rssi;
    while (true)
    {
        sleep_ms(1000);
        cyw43_wifi_get_rssi(&cyw43_state, &rssi);
        printf("rssi: %d \n", rssi);
    }
}
```

Remember to include the usual CMakeLists.txt, lwipopts.h and setupWifi.h in this program.

The get_rssi function uses an ioctl call and you can replace it by the equivalent:

```
cyw43_ioctl(&cyw43_state, CYW43_IOCTL_GET_RSSI,
        sizeof(rssi), (uint8_t*)&rssi, CYW43_ITF_STA);
```

As ioctl calls are usually undocumented, the problem with them is discovering exactly what the commands are and what they do.

Summary

- The Pico W uses an Infineon CYW43439, which has a pair of ARM processors, connected to the Pico via a simple 3-wire SPI bus.

- To avoid having to use GPIO lines in SPI mode, the driver makes use of one of the PIOs to implement the protocol. It also uses GPIO 25 to generate interrupts when the hardware needs servicing.

- The pico's wifi stack is composed of a number of different layers starting with the CYW43 driver.

- The driver has a lower-level module cyw43_ll which deals directly with the hardware.

- There are three different ways to operate the WiFi – polling, interrupts or Free RTOS.

- Polling mode is free from the possibility of race conditions, but you have to call a polling function on a regular basis.

- Interrupt mode works without you having to implement polling, but you have to use locking to protect against race conditions.

- Free RTOS mode involves adopting an operating system, which is a lot to do simply to gain access to WiFi. If you do use Free RTOS, however, you can use sockets.

- Interrupt mode only supports the raw lwIP API which works using callbacks. It is easy to use, but it involves locking.

- The latest SDK uses async contexts to organize locking.

- It is worth creating and using a standard WiFi connect or setup function.

- The NETIF lwIP module provides a connection to the raw network interface.

- NETIF allows you to implement a scan of available WiFi access points.

Chapter 2
Introduction To TCP

Once you have used the WiFi driver to connect to a network the next problem is how to implement the many network protocols that are in use. The Pico SDK comes with the lwIP (lightweight Internet Protocol) library that is ready to use. IP is a low-level protocol that supports a number of other higher-level protocols on top and of these TCP (Transmission Control Protocol) is the most commonly used because it is the basis of how web clients and servers communicate. In this chapter we look at how to use lwIP to work with TCP. If you are interested in using lwIP to implement a web client, this is covered in *Programming The Raspberry Pi Pico/W in C, 2nd Ed*, where we used one of the high-level applications supplied in the library. In this chapter we use the lower level raw TCP library which gives more control over how everything works and allows the addition of SSL/TSL (Secure Sockets Layer/Transport Layer Security) encryption and security.

Ethernet, IP, TCP and HTTP

It isn't entirely necessary to understand the details of how modern networking is organized, but a rough idea helps. At this point most accounts would introduce the OSI (Open Systems Interconnection) model, but this is more than the working programmer needs to know. In practice, there is just one common lower-level, Ethernet, and on top of that we have IP (Internet Protocol).

Most computers are physically connected together by Ethernet networks. This is a packet-switched network, which means that data is transmitted in chunks called packets and each packet has the address of the machine it is being sent to and the address of the machine that sent it. For Ethernet the addresses are called MAC (Media Access Control) addresses. These are 48-bit unique identifiers. When anyone manufactures an Ethernet interface they apply for a unique MAC address for it. This means that in principle every machine on an Ethernet network has a unique MAC address. This can be useful if you need a unique identifier for other purposes and a machine's MAC address is often used to create a 128-bit GUID (Globally Unique IDentifier) by incorporating the exact date and time. Some devices, such as routers, have software definable MAC addresses for various reasons and this does spoil the simple picture. However, in the main you can regard a MAC address as being effectively unique.

Ethernet packets are sent from their source to their destination on the basis of the MAC address specified. The hardware that makes up the network, usually switches, learns which machines are connected on which ports by monitoring network traffic and send the packets to the correct destination.

The problem with the MAC address is that it isn't routable. You cannot take a MAC address and work out that the destination is on some other network and send the packet there for further routing. All of the machines that are reachable by Ethernet packets are essentially on the same physical network. Ethernet is a local area networking protocol.

The IP address is, however, routable and it was designed to be so. An IP data packet uses IP addresses rather than MAC addresses, even though the packets are actually transported within Ethernet packets complete with MAC addresses. The network software resolves the IP address to a local MAC address and then the Ethernet takes care of delivery to the destination machine where the IP packet is removed from the Ethernet packet and passed to higher-level software. The matching up of IP addresses and MAC addresses is done by a protocol called the Address Resolution Protocol, ARP. As long as the IP address can be resolved to a local MAC address, delivery is simple and direct via the network switches.

When an IP address is used that doesn't correspond to a local address, i.e. one not on the specified sub-net, then the packet is sent to the designated router and it is expected to send the packet on to other routers which will see it safely delivered to the correct network. In principle, IP networking can sit on top of any hardware-implemented network and not just Ethernet.

Mostly you can ignore the Ethernet component of the network apart from the occasional need to know about or work with a MAC address. The IP component, however, is much more important and is what you work with most of the time. This is a raw packet switching protocol which simply sends packets to their destinations without needing to know anything about what is in them. On top of IP you can create other protocols. The simplest is UDP (User Datagram Protocol) which basically allows you to send packets of data to one or more recipients without error correction or even any guarantees of delivery. UDP is a fast but unreliable data transfer protocol. Another protocol built on IP is TCP (Transmission Control Protocol)TCP is less efficient than UDP, but it provides a reliable connection with error correction and guarantees not only delivery of each packet but delivery in the correct order. TCP is the protocol used to transfer web pages between client and server and it is a completely general data transfer protocol.

When transferring web pages yet another protocol is employed to control exactly what data is transferred. The HTTP (HyperText Transfer Protocol) is a set of requests that determine what data a client and a server will exchange. It is transported as the data within a TCP connection.

Now that we know how things work, the usual network layer diagram should make sense:

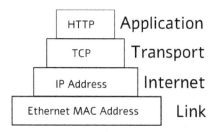

To recap:

- IP packets are transferred on the local network within Ethernet packets which are sent from source to destination using MAC addresses.

- IP packets can be routed outside of the local network via a router. The source and destination are specified using an IP address and the IP address is mapped to a MAC address once the packet reaches the local network.

- UDP is a simple protocol that uses IP packets to send datagrams without error checking or assured delivery.

- TCP uses IP packets to transfer metadata that the software can use to ensure a reliable connection including error correction and tests for data integrity.

- HTTP uses a TCP connection to send requests for particular data or actions to be performed.

In principle each of these layers could be changed, but in practice only the Application and Transport layers vary significantly in practice.

Understanding the different network layers helps you understand the way the lwIP library is structured. Without an operating system the Pico is restricted to RAW APIs, which are based on callbacks rather than threading. The different RAW modules that are available are organized by the protocols they support:

- Ethernet
  used to send an Ethernet packet to a MAC address

- IP
  implements the IP protocol and allows you to send a basic IP packet formatted as you like and to access to some basic IP protocols such as DHCP which controls IP address assignment and IGMP which is used for multicast transmission control

- ◆ TCP
  implements TCP using the IP module
- ◆ UDP
  implements UDP using the IP module

In addition there is a DNS module which implements a DNS resolver, which is an application layer protocol usually transmitted using UDP. There are also modules designed to make working with IP addresses easier, but note that the Pico only supports IPv4.

TCP

We could start at a lower level in the stack, but TCP is the most commonly encountered transport protocol and it is used to implement web clients and web servers among other things, so it is a good practical level to start.

A TCP data exchange has to be made via a connection made by a client to a server. The client asks to connect to the server and the server accepts or rejects the connection. Once the connection has been made data can flow from client to server or vice versa. Connections are specified and controlled using a PCB, Protocol Control Block. What usually happens is that you first create a PCB and then use this to accept or make a connection. Once you have a connection data can be sent and received. The PCB is used to keep track of the state of the connection, including storing any data while it is being transferred and to customize the TCP protocol.

Creating a PCB

To create a PCB you use:

```
pcb= tcp_new();
```

Next you have to initialize the pcb. It has a set of fields that record the callbacks that are used to service the data transfer. You need to use access functions to set the callbacks rather than setting the fields directly.

- ◆ tcp_sent(pcb, sent);

  The sent function is called when the remote side of the connection has acknowledged the data sent to it. You can use this to free resources and to detect when the PCB has freed up space in its data storage and you can send more data. The signature of the sent function has to be:

  ```
  err_t sent(void *arg, struct pcb *pcb, u16_t len)
  ```

  where pcb is the PCB that sent the data and len is the number of bytes sent. The first parameter, arg, is a custom argument that you can specify to be sent to the callback and it is included in all of the callbacks.

- tcp_recv(pcb, recv);

The recv function is called when data is ready to be proceeded by the client.

The signature of the recv function is:

```
errr_t recv(void *arg, struct tcp_pcb *pcb,
                            struct pbuf *p, err_t err)
```

where pcb is the PCB that received the data, p is a PBUF which contains the data and err_t is an error code associated with the received data and used if there was a transmission error. The PBUF is a data structure in the form of a linked list that holds the packets transmitted over the connection. There are some utility functions that make working with a PBUF easy, see later. However, you should call:

```
void tcp_recved(pcb,len)
```

after the received data has been retrieved and is no longer wanted in order to free up the len bytes in the PCB for more data.

- tcp_err(pcb, err);

The err function called if there is any error associated with the PCB. Not all errors result in this function being called, some are reported to a more appropriate callback, but it is called when a connection receives a RST (reset) instruction from the server or when it is unexpectedly closed.

Making the Connection

The PCB is all about implementing the connection, but it isn't involved in determining where the connection is to. Exactly how the connection is made depends on whether you are the client or the server. For simplicity we will deal with how a client connects first and come back to the problem of handling server connections.

A client connection is made using the tcp_connect function. This is where you specify the IP address and port number for the connection:

```
err_t tcp_connect(struct tcp_pcb * pcb,
                  const ip_addr_t * ipaddr, u16_t port,
                            tcp_connected_fn connected )
```

The pcb is the PCB used for the connection and hence it specifies the callback functions. The ipaddr and port specify the server and the connected function is called when the connection is made.

Its signature is:

```
err_t connected(void *arg, struct _pcb *pcb, err_t err)
```

where pcb specifies the PCB used in the connection.

The err parameter is currently unused and it is always ERR_OK. If there is an error the error callback set up in the PCB is called. The first parameter, arg, is a custom argument that you can set to be passed to all callbacks associated with the PCB.

Once you have an open connection you can send data to the server using:

```
err_t tcp_write(struct tcp_pcb *pcb,
                const void * data, u16_t len u8_t apiflags)
```

where pcb specifies the PCB to use, data is a pointer to the data to be sent and len specifies the number of bytes in the data buffer.

Finally apiflags specifies how the data should be treated and can be

- TCP_WRITE_FLAG_COPY
  specifies that the data buffer should be copied into internal stack memory. If you don't specify this the buffer that you supply should not be changed until the data has been transmitted and acknowledged.

- TCP_WRITE_FLAG_MORE
  indicates that more data follows.

The amount of data sent should not exceed the limit defined in the lwipopts.h file. If there isn't enough memory the function returns ERR_MEM. You can find out the size of the internal buffer using the tcp_sndbuf() macro.

The data isn't always sent immediately and you should call:

```
err_t tcp_output(struct tcp_pcb *pcb)
```

specifying the appropriate PCB to ensure it is sent.

There are other useful TCP functions but these are all we need to write a simple HTTP client. The basic algorithm is:

1. Create and initialize a PCB with at least a recv callback defined

2. Use tcp_connect to connect to a specified IP and port address and supply a connected callback

3. Create the connected callback to send data to the server and create the recv callback to process the data that the server sends back in response.

HTTP

The simplest way to make use of a WiFi connection is to work with an HTTP server. This is simple because the difficult parts of the transaction are handled by the server, making the client much easier to implement.

Using what we know so far about raw TCP, we can easily connect to a server and send and receive data. What data we actually send and receive depends on the protocol in use. Web servers use HTTP, which is a very simple text-based protocol.

The HTTP protocol is essentially a set of text headers of the form:

headername: *headerdata* \r\n

that tell the server what to do, and a set of headers that the server sends back to tell you what it has done. There are very many HTTP headers and you can look up their details of in the documentation.

The most important header is the very first which acts as a command to tell the server what the client wants to do – a client request. HTTP supports a number of request methods which transfer data. Usually these are described in terms of what they do to resources hosted by a web server, but from our point of view what matters is what happens to the data.

The HTTP request methods available are:

GET	Transfers data from server to client
HEAD	Transfers HTTP headers for the equivalent GET request
PUT	Transfers data from the client to the server
POST	Transfers data from the client to the server
PATCH	Transfers data from the client to the server
DELETE	Specifies that the data on the server should be deleted
OPTIONS	Transfers data from the client to the server

If you know about HTTP request methods you will find the above list disconcerting. If you don't know about HTTP requests then you will be wondering why there are so many requests that transfer data from the client to the server? The answer is that in the HTTP model the server stores the master copy of the resource – usually a file or a database entry. The client can request a copy of the resource using GET and then ask the server to modify the resource using the other requests. For example, the PUT request sends a new copy of the resource for the server to use, i.e. it replaces the old copy. POST does the same thing, but PUT should be idempotent which means that if you repeat it the result is as if you had done it just once. With POST you are allowed side effects. For example, PUT 1 might just store 1 but POST 1 might increment a count.

Another example is where you sends some text to the server to save under a supplied file name. For this you should use a PUT as repeating the request with the same text changes nothing. If, on the other hand, you supply text to the server and allow it to assign a name and store it then you should use a POST as you get a new file each time you send the data, even it is the same.

Similarly the PATCH request should be used by the client to request that that server makes a change to part of an existing resource. Exactly how the change is specified depends on the server. Usually a key value scheme is used, but this isn't part of the specification.

Notice that all of these interpretations of the HTTP request methods are "optional" in the sense that it is up to you and the server you are using to interpret and implement them. If you write your own server, or server application, then you can treat POST as if it was PUT and vice versa.

A Custom Test Server

The problem with writing HTTP examples is that how they are handled depends on the server in use. Not all HTTP servers implement the same range of requests. A simple solution to this problem is to write a custom server and switching to Python makes this very easy. Before you try any of the following examples, create the following Python program on a suitable machine on your local network, the code can be downloaded from the book's web page. Notice that this code is Python 3.10 or later:

```python
from http.server import HTTPServer, BaseHTTPRequestHandler
from io import BytesIO

class SimpleHTTPRequestHandler(BaseHTTPRequestHandler):

    def sendResponse(self, cmd):
        content_length = int(self.headers['Content-Length'])
        body = self.rfile.read(content_length)
        self.send_response(200)
        self.end_headers()
        response = BytesIO()
        response.write(b'This is a '+bytes(cmd, 'utf-8')+
                                                b' request. ')
        response.write(b'Received: ')
        response.write(body)
        self.wfile.write(response.getvalue())
```

```
def do_GET(self):
 self.send_response(200)
 self.end_headers()
 self.wfile.write(b'Hello, world!')

 def do_HEAD(self):
 self.send_response(200)
 self.end_headers()

 def do_POST(self):
 self.sendResponse("POST")

 def do_PUT(self):
 self.sendResponse("PUT")

 def do_DELETE(self):
 self.sendResponse("DELETE")

 def do_PATCH(self):
 self.sendResponse("PATCH")

httpd = HTTPServer(('', 8080), SimpleHTTPRequestHandler)
httpd.serve_forever()
```

This server implements simple methods to respond to GET, HEAD, PUT, POST, DELETE and PATCH requests. If you want to support a custom request simply include a method that is called do_request where request is the command you want to use.

Notice that this custom request is unlikely to be serviced by a standard server, but there is nothing stopping you from implementing your own. In the case of GET, the server sends fixed data – "Hello World" - and for the others it sends back whatever was sent to it by the client, with the exception of HEAD that sends nothing at all except for the headers.

If you install this program on a remote machine on the same network as the Pico then you can use it to test HTTP request programs. With a little work you can also turn it into a server that supports your Pico app in the external world. You can even convert it into a TLS/ SSL server for HTTPS connections using the Python SSL module.

An HTTP Client

As a first example we can construct the simplest possible HTTP client. In the sake of simplicity no error checking is performed and only the callbacks that are needed are defined. This is as simple as it gets and a starting point for a more complete client.

The most basic transaction the client can have with the server is to send a GET request for the server to send back a particular file. Thus the simplest header is:

```
"GET /index.html HTTP/1.1\r\n\r\n"
```

which is a request for the server to send index.html. In most cases we need one more header, HOST, which gives the domain name of the server. Why do we need it? Simply because HTTP says you should and many websites are hosted by a single server at the same IP address. Which website the server retrieves the file from is governed by the domain name you specify in the HOST header.

This means that the simplest set of headers we can send the server is:

```
"GET /index.htm HTTP/1.1\r\nHOST:example.org\r\n\r\"
```

which corresponds to the headers:

```
GET /index.html HTTP/1.1
HOST:example.org
```

An HTTP request always ends with a blank line. If you don't send the blank line then you will get no response from most servers. In addition, the HOST header has to have the domain name with no additional syntax - no slashes and no http: or similar.

```
#define BUF_SIZE 2048
char myBuff[BUF_SIZE];
char header[] =
          "GET /index.html HTTP/1.1\r\nHOST:example.com\r\n\r\n";
```

Now we are ready to send our request to the server and the first thing we need is a PCB set to call a recv callback:

```
struct tcp_pcb *pcb = tcp_new();
tcp_recv(pcb, recv);
```

In this case we only need to define a callback to handle the received data. Now we have a PCB we can connect to the server:

```
ip_addr_t ip;
IP4_ADDR(&ip, 93, 184, 216, 34);
cyw43_arch_lwip_begin();
err_t err = tcp_connect(pcb, &ip, 80, connected);
cyw43_arch_lwip_end();
```

Now all we have to do is define the two callbacks. The connected callback is used to send the headers to the server:

```
static err_t connected(void *arg, struct tcp_pcb *pcb, err_t err)
{
    err = tcp_write(pcb, header, strlen(header), 0);
    err = tcp_output(pcb);
    return ERR_OK;
}
```

The recv callback simply checks to see that there really is something to read and then displays some statistics, converts the PBUF to a character array and displays the content. Finally it reports that the data has been received and frees the PBUF.

```
err_t recv(void *arg, struct tcp_pcb *pcb,
                                  struct pbuf *p, err_t err)
{
 if (p != NULL)
 {
    printf("recv total %d  this buffer %d next %d err %d\n",
                          p->tot_len, p->len, p->next, err);
    pbuf_copy_partial(p, myBuff, p->tot_len, 0);
    myBuff[p->tot_len] = 0;
    printf("Buffer= %s\n", myBuff);
    tcp_recved(pcb, p->tot_len);
    pbuf_free(p);
 }
 return ERR_OK;
}
```

This is a very simple receive function and it doesn't make any attempt to deal with empty responses from the server or to close the connection.

Usually an HTTP 1.1 connection is left open even after the requested data has been transmitted by the server just in case it can be reused by the client for another request. In this case the connection eventually times out. You can include an additional header Connection: close to ask the server not to keep the connection open but some will ignore this.

The complete program is:

```c
#include <stdio.h>
#include "pico/stdlib.h"
#include "pico/cyw43_arch.h"
#include "setupWifi.h"
#include "lwip/tcp.h"

#define BUF_SIZE 2048
char myBuff[BUF_SIZE];
char header[] =
  "GET /index.html HTTP/1.1\r\n
        HOST:example.com\r\n";

err_t recv(void *arg, struct tcp_pcb *pcb,
                              struct pbuf *p, err_t err)
{
 if (p != NULL)
 {
    printf("recv total %d  this buffer %d next %d err %d\n",
                        p->tot_len, p->len, p->next, err);
    pbuf_copy_partial(p, myBuff, p->tot_len, 0);
    myBuff[p->tot_len] = 0;
    printf("Buffer= %s\n", myBuff);
    tcp_recved(pcb, p->tot_len);
    pbuf_free(p);
 }
 return ERR_OK;
}

err_t connected(void *arg, struct tcp_pcb *pcb, err_t err)
{
 err = tcp_write(pcb, header, strlen(header), 0);
 err = tcp_output(pcb);
 return ERR_OK;
}

int main()
{
    stdio_init_all();
    connect();
    struct tcp_pcb *pcb = tcp_new();
    tcp_recv(pcb, recv);
    ip_addr_t ip;
    IP4_ADDR(&ip, 93, 184, 216, 34);
    cyw43_arch_lwip_begin();
    err_t err = tcp_connect(pcb, &ip, 80, connected);
    cyw43_arch_lwip_end();
```

```
while (true)
    {
        sleep_ms(500);
    }
}
```

The `CmakeLists.txt` file is as before:

```
cmake_minimum_required(VERSION 3.13)
set(PICO_BOARD pico_w)
set(CMAKE_C_STANDARD 11)
set(CMAKE_CXX_STANDARD 17)

include(pico_sdk_import.cmake)
project(PicoW C CXX ASM)
pico_sdk_init()

add_executable(main
 main.c
)

target_include_directories(main PRIVATE ${CMAKE_CURRENT_LIST_DIR})
target_link_libraries(main pico_stdlib
                        pico_cyw43_arch_lwip_threadsafe_background)
pico_add_extra_outputs(main)
```

and you also need the default `lwipopts.h`, `pico_sdk_import.cmake`.
`launch.json` and of course `setupWifi.h` given in a previous chapter. If you
run the program you will see the headers and HTML that makes up the page
at example.com. You will also notice that the page is sent using more than
one packet.

Many improvements could be included to finish this simple program, but
first we need to convert the program from the TCP module to the
Application Layered module.

The Application Layered Module

If you are sure that all you will want to do is use a standard TCP connection
you can use the TCP module as in the previous example. However, it is often
that case that you need to use a modified TCP connection and this is where
the Application Layered TCP (ALTCP) module comes into play. In particular,
the ALTCP module is needed if you want to use an TLS/SSL TCP
connection.

The basic idea is that the ALTCP module provides all of the functions in the
TCP module, but they can be easily substituted by alternative
implementations at run time.

This means you can write your TCP application using the ALTCP module and later use an alternative implementation of TCP. In most cases there is nothing to lose by using ALTCP and a great deal of flexibility to be gained. All of the examples in the rest of this book make use of it, but you can easily change the programs to use the TCP module.

There are five changes needed to use the ALTCP module.

1. Replace the `tcp.h` header by `alttcp.h`
2. Replace `tcp_` by `alttcp_` in all of the functions.
3. Use struct `altcp_pcb` in place of struct `tcp_pcb` for the PCB.
4. The `altcp_new` function takes a parameter, `altcp_allocator_t`, which holds the state of whatever alternative TCP connection is in use. If you are using a standard TCP connection then you can pass `NULL` as the allocator.
5. Set `LWIP_ALTCP` to `1` in the `lwipopts.h` file. If you don't, the program will be compiled against the TCP module and while it will work you won't be able to specify an alternative TCP connection.

Notice that this allows you to set the type of TCP connection at run time by passing a suitable allocator.

Applying these changes to the previous example gives us a simple HTTP client using ALTCP:

```
#include <stdio.h>
#include "pico/stdlib.h"
#include "pico/cyw43_arch.h"
#include "setupWifi.h"
#include "lwip/altcp.h"


#define BUF_SIZE 2048
char myBuff[BUF_SIZE];
char header[] = "GET /index.html HTTP/1.1\r\n
                        HOST:example.com\r\n\r\n";
err_t recv(void *arg, struct altcp_pcb *pcb,
                                struct pbuf *p, err_t err)
{
 if (p != NULL)
 {
     printf("recv total %d  this buffer %d next %d err %d\n",
                        p->tot_len, p->len, p->next, err);
     pbuf_copy_partial(p, myBuff, p->tot_len, 0);
     myBuff[p->tot_len] = 0;
     printf("Buffer= %s\n", myBuff);
     altcp_recved(pcb, p->tot_len);
     pbuf_free(p);
 }
     return ERR_OK;
}
```

```
static err_t connected(void *arg, struct altcp_pcb *pcb, err_t err)
{
    err = altcp_write(pcb, header, strlen(header), 0);
    err = altcp_output(pcb);
    return ERR_OK;
}

int main()
{
    stdio_init_all();
    connect();

    struct altcp_pcb *pcb = altcp_new(NULL);
    altcp_recv(pcb, recv);

    ip_addr_t ip;
    IP4_ADDR(&ip, 93, 184, 216, 34);
    cyw43_arch_lwip_begin();
    err_t err = altcp_connect(pcb, &ip, 80, connected);
    cyw43_arch_lwip_end();

    while (true)
    {
        sleep_ms(500);
    }
}
```

This compiles with no other changes, but if you want to actually make use of the ALTCP module you have to add:

```
#define LWIP_ALTCP              1
```

to the lwipopts.h file. With this change you will need a clean rebuild before it will work.

A More Practical Client

The first thing that most more developed HTTP clients do is define an error and a sent callback:

```
struct altcp_pcb *pcb = altcp_new(NULL);
altcp_recv(pcb, recv);
altcp_sent(pcb, sent);
altcp_err(pcb, err);
```

Basic implementations of each callback could be something like:

```
err_t sent(void *arg, struct altcp_pcb *pcb, u16_t len)
{
    printf("data sent %d\n", len);
}

void err(void *arg, err_t err)
{
    if (err != ERR_ABRT)
    {
        printf("client_err %d\n", err);
    }
}
```

A more pressing need is the ability to detect when the data transfer is complete and the connection is closed or needs closing. At the moment the program simply keeps the connection open for as long as the server keeps it open. The recv callback is called with a NULL pointer to a PBUF when the connection has been closed. This means that we can deal with a connection closure using:

```
err_t recv(void *arg, struct altcp_pcb *pcb,
                                    struct pbuf *p, err_t err)
{
    if (p != NULL)
    {
        printf("recv total %d  this buffer %d next %d err %d\n",
                            p->tot_len, p->len, p->next, err);
        if ((p->tot_len) > 2)
        {
            pbuf_copy_partial(p, myBuff, p->tot_len, 0);
            myBuff[p->tot_len] = 0;
            printf("Buffer= %s\n", myBuff);
            altcp_recved(pcb, p->tot_len);
        }
        pbuf_free(p);
    }else
    {
        printf("Connection Closed");
        altcp_close(pcb);
    }
    return ERR_OK;
}
```

There is also an if statement that takes account of the fact that servers often send empty packets or packets with just a blank line. If you try this out you will discover that the connection is closed, but only when the server finally times out and closes it. The problem is that HTTP 1.1 allows servers to keep a connection open so that it could be used for another request. If you want to close the connection faster than this – because you know that the client isn't going to make another request – then there are two possible ways of dealing with the problem. The first is to make use of the poll callback. This is called if the connection is idle for a specified timeout. To set the poll callback you use:

```
void altcp_poll(pcb, poll, interval)
```

The interval is the timeout in terms of TCP timer intervals which are usually half seconds. The signature of the poll callback is:

```
err_t poll(void *arg, struct tcp_pcb *tpcb)
```

For example, to close the connection after 5 seconds of idle you would use:

```
altcp_poll(pcb, poll,10);
```

and define the poll callback as:

```
err_t poll(void *arg, struct altcp_pcb *pcb){
        printf("Connection Closed");
        altcp_close(pcb);
}
```

If you make this modification and run the program you will find that the connection is closed after five seconds of the web page being displayed. The poll callback can be used for any task that needs to be performed if the connection is idle.

An alternative to using the poll callback is to ask the server to close the connection, using the Connection header, when the request is complete. This works on its own and in conjunction with the poll callback just in case the server doesn't honor the header. To do this you simply have to add to the header string:

```
char header[] = "GET /index.html HTTP/1.1\r\n
                HOST:example.com\r\n
                    Connection: close\r\n\r\n";
```

If you try this out you should find that the connection is closed as soon as the web page is displayed.

Summary

- Networks transfer data between devices as packets, complete with source and destination address.

- Ethernet is a low-level protocol which is used to transfer packets between machines connected to a local network. Each machine has a unique MAC address which is used to determine where a packet should be sent.

- Ethernet isn't a routable protocol in the sense that MAC addresses give no clue as to where a machine might be located.

- IP is a routable protocol which means it can be used to send packets to distant networks.

- IP is usually transferred within Ethernet packets and IP addresses are converted to MAC addresses using ARP. If an IP address is not found on the local network then the packet is sent to a router, which passes it on to other networks.

- The IP protocol is used to implement higher-level protocols such as UDP and TCP.

- In their turn these higher-level protocols are used to implement protocols which transfer larger units of data such as HTTP which uses TCP to transfer web pages.

- The lwIP library is structured according to the same protocol levels into modules. As we are not using Free RTOS, the RAW API is the one to use and it works in terms of callbacks.

- The TCP module works in terms of PCBs Protocol Control Blocks to specify the callbacks to be used and the state of the connection.

- The basic procedure is to create and initialize a PCB with at least a receive callback defined then connect to a specified IP and port address and supply a connected callback to send data back to the server. The receive callback then processes the data.

- HTTP defines actions such as GET and PUT which retrieve a file from the server or send a file to the server respectively.

- If you want to modify the connection protocol, e.g. replace HTTP by HTTPS then you should use the Application Layer TCP which works in the same way as the TCP module.

Chapter 3

More Advanced TCP

Getting a simple HTTP client working is a good first step, but it is still a long way from making use of HTTP within an application. The main problem is how to integrate the asynchronous operation of networking with the rest of the program. The simplest situation is where whatever your program is doing isn't time critical and you can wait until a network connection has been established and the data sent and received. In this situation you can implement your networking functions as blocking, i.e. they do not return until the task is complete.

If you have to keep the program active while waiting for network tasks to complete then you can't adopt this simple blocking approach. Instead your networking functions have to be non-blocking, i.e. they have to return at once and you need to implement a mechanism that lets you know when the task is complete. lwIP in raw mode solves this problem using callbacks, but this is not an ideal way to structure your code. In this chapter we look at ways of incorporating callbacks into your main program without distorting its logic and at more advanced uses of TCP in client mode.

The Callback Problem

The biggest challenge in using the RAW TCP module with callbacks is the callbacks. It is well known that callbacks are a problem in that they distort the usual flow of control. You might want to write code that downloads a web page and then processes the data, but callbacks force you to write that as a download which calls a callback which processes the data. Once the callback has started it logically becomes the "main" function in your program in the sense it is where everything has to happen. Code that would have been in the main flow of your program is now stuck into a callback function and possibly multiple callback functions.

For example, you simply want to send a request to a server and get some data back. Logically your program is:

```
void main(){
      doconnect();
      dosend();
      doread();
      doprocess();
}
```

where each function call is assumed to be blocking and only returns when it has completed its task.

However, we already know that you can't send data to a server until the connection is made and the connected callback is called. So the connected callback has to send the data. Similarly the reception of data results in the recv callback being called and hence this is where you read the data. This leaves the question of where you process the data? In the recv callback? In the main program? The simple logical flow of control in the blocking version has been converted into:

```
void connect(){
      dosend();
}
void recv(){
      doprocess();
}
void main(){
      doconnect();
}
```

Now the only action visible in the main program is the connection – everything else happens in callbacks. This makes the logic of the program very difficult to understand and hence get right. Of course, the advantage is that the main program is free to get on with other tasks after it has handed off responsibility for the interaction with the server to the callbacks. For example:

```
void connect(){
      dosend();
}
void recv(){
      doprocess();
}
void main(){
      doconnect();
      while(true){
            toggle(led);
      }
}
```

flashes an LED as the interaction with the server proceeds. How would you achieve this with the blocking version of the program?

This is bad enough, but there is an even more important problem. The callbacks run in the same context as the lwIP functions. That is while the callback is running the other lwIP functions, including the WiFi driver are blocked. This means that ideally your callback should get its job done quickly and give the execution context back to lwIP and the WiFi driver.

Even if you can get the job done quickly, there is the secondary difficulty of dealing with the multiple packets that the data might be delivered in. For example, if you are downloading a web page to extract data from it then the first time that the receive callback is called the whole web page may not be available. Indeed there may be no time that the callback has access to the entire web page data as it is called when there is a fragment of data available. This makes the logic of the program even more distorted as now the recv callback cannot simply call the processing function as it has to work out when the data transfer is complete, i.e. it will potentially be called multiple times before needing to call doprocess.

This is the reason that the lwIP documentation says that the RAW callback approach is very efficient, but at the cost of being easy to use. There are advanced approaches to make using callbacks easier, notably Promises and Async/Await constructs in other languages. For C and for small systems like the Pico these are not efficient and they are not common. A simpler solution is to use a state-based approach – and this is what the first parameter, arg, of all of the lwIP callbacks is for.

State

The simple idea is to use a state variable to indicate what is happening with the data transfer and allow the main program to wait for each state in turn before moving the process on. This makes the state polling loop the central structure for your application. This polling loop repeatedly checks on what is happening with the WiFi and at the same time carries out the other operations you need to support – flashing an LED, reading sensors and so on. The main polling loop is the best way to structure your program in the absence of a multithreaded operating system.

For example, our previous LED flashing client program could be written:

```
void connect(){
      state=connected;
}
void recv(){
      state=dataready;
}
void main(){
      state=notconnected;
      doconnect();
      while(true){
            if(connected)dosend();
            if(dataready)doprocess();
            toggle(led);
      }
}
```

Now you can see all of the logical steps of the process in the main program – they are not in a fixed sequential order, but this is a reflection of the fact that the program is asynchronous and things can happen in any order. In this approach the callbacks are used to change the state variable so that the main program can move on to the next stage of processing. This makes the callbacks very lightweight and unlikely to slow the driver or lwIP down.

A State-Driven Client

It turns out to be slightly more complicated than you might expect to implement a state-based method, but let's try a simple approach first by defining a global integer state variable:

```
int state = 0;
```

with the following interpretation:

State	Meaning
0	not connected
1	connecting
2	connected
3	request pending
4	initial data packet
5	waiting for more data
6	data ready for processing

The choice of states is always a difficult one and you can always add more. For example, in a real situation there should be an error state.

The state variable can be passed to each of the callbacks so that they can set it appropriately:

```
int state = 0;
altcp_arg(pcb, &state);
```

All we need to is set the state variable and test its value in the final polling loop:

```
 ip_addr_t ip;
    IP4_ADDR(&ip, 93, 184, 216, 34);
    cyw43_arch_lwip_begin();
    err_t err = altcp_connect(pcb, &ip, 80, connected);
    cyw43_arch_lwip_end();
    state = 1;

    while (state != 0)
    {
        switch (state)
        {
        case 0:
        case 1:
        case 3:
            break;
        case 2:
            state = 3;
            cyw43_arch_lwip_begin();
            err = altcp_write(pcb, header, strlen(header), 0);
            err = altcp_output(pcb);
            cyw43_arch_lwip_end();
            break;
        case 4:
            state = 5;
            break;
        case 6:
            printf("Buffer= %s\n", myBuff);
            state = 0;
            break;
        default:
            sleep_ms(1000);
            printf("LED Flash\n");
        }
    }
    printf("Data Transferred\n");
```

You could include any other non-networking tasks that need to be performed within this polling loop, but for an example this simply displays LED Flash at one second intervals. A switch is used, but you can use a set of if statements if you need to check more complex state conditions. You can see that some of the states involve doing nothing in the polling loop, others trigger an action and other simply change the state.

The callbacks now mainly just set the state variable:

```
err_t recv(void *arg, struct altcp_pcb *pcb,
                              struct pbuf *p, err_t err)
{
 if (p != NULL)
 {
    printf("recv total %d  this buffer %d next %d err %d\n",
                       p->tot_len, p->len, p->next, err);
      if ((p->tot_len) > 2)
      {
        pbuf_copy_partial(p, myBuff, p->tot_len, 0);
        myBuff[p->tot_len] = 0;
        *(int *)arg = 4;
        altcp_recved(pcb, p->tot_len);
      }
    pbuf_free(p);
 }
 else
 {
    printf("Connection Closed \n");
    altcp_close(pcb);
    *(int *)arg = 6;
 }
 return ERR_OK;
}

static err_t connected(void *arg, struct altcp_pcb *pcb, err_t err)
{
    *(int *)arg = 2;
    return ERR_OK;
}
err_t poll(void *arg, struct altcp_pcb *pcb)
{
    printf("Connection Closed \n");
    *(int *)arg = 6;
    altcp_close(pcb);
}
```

The state variable is passed as the `arg` parameter, but as this is a pointer to void it has to be cast to the correct type, i.e. `(int *)arg` pointer to `int` before use.

If you make these modifications and try it out you will find that it almost works. The program, a complete version of which can be found on the book's web page, goes through the states, but the final buffer only contains the data from the final packet. We need to save all of the data in the buffer, not just have the most recent packet overwrite what is already in the buffer. It is clear that the state variable needs to record more information about how far the transaction has progressed.

Another problem with our design is that the state variable is global. This restricts our network use to one operation at a time. For example, we can only start a single web page downloading at a time because we have only a single state variable to track the state of a single network transaction. If we want to allow for the possibility of more than one network operation at a time we need to implement something more sophisticated.

State Struct

A much better approach is to use a state struct and incorporate all of the data needed for the state of the connection. This is the approach often used by initial examples and it makes understanding what is happening more difficult specially when they don't use a state-based approach. Having explored the problem you should be able to see that this is a good approach, even if it is more complicated.

The first thing we need is a struct to hold the current state:

```
struct connectionState {
 int state;
 struct altcp_pcb *pcb;
 char *myBuff;
 int start;
};
```

You can record any information that you consider relevant and useful in connectionState but keep in mind that there are some things that are general to connections and specific to a particular connection. For example, you can reuse the same connectionState struct with different IP addresses and different requests so these are probably best not stored in connectionState. In this case we have chosen to record the state variable we used in the previous example, the PCB, a buffer for the data and a pointer to the start of the free space in the buffer.

Once you have the connectionState struct it makes sense to create a function to initialize it and the PCB field it contains:

```
err_t newConnection(struct connectionState *cs, char *buf){
    cs->state=0;
    cs->pcb = altcp_new(NULL);
    altcp_recv(cs->pcb, recv);
    altcp_sent(cs->pcb, sent);
    altcp_err(cs->pcb, err);
    altcp_poll(cs->pcb, poll, 10);
    altcp_arg(cs->pcb, cs);
    cs->myBuff=buf;
    cs->start=0;
    return ERR_OK;
}
```

You can see that this function creates a new PCB and sets up the callbacks. It also sets the pointer to the buffer to be used by the recv callback. Notice that the connectionState has to be passed in – this saves having to allocate it on the heap and remembering to deallocate it later. On the other hand, allocating the buffer on the heap and providing a cleanup function for the struct is another good alternative.

The start field is used to keep track of where to store new data in the buffer. Also notice that we are now setting cs as a custom argument to be passed to all of the callbacks. This also allows the callbacks to be tied to a particular instance of the connectionState struct, which means they can be reused for multiple network operations. That is, the connectionState struct tells each callback which particular network operation it has been called to deal with. This allows us to define one set of callbacks that can be reused with any network operation and this, in turn, allows us to abstract them from our use of the network.

Another modification is to refactor the WiFi state management from the polling loop in the main program to a more general function. After all, the main program really doesn't care about the states that the WiFi goes through except when the data is ready, i.e. when state == 6.

```
int pollConnection(struct connectionState *cs)
{
    switch (cs->state)
    {
    case 0:
    case 1:
    case 3:
    case 6:
        break;
    case 2:
        cs->state = 3;
        cyw43_arch_lwip_begin();
        err_t err = altcp_write(cs->pcb, header,
                                        strlen(header), 0);
        err = altcp_output(cs->pcb);
        cyw43_arch_lwip_end();
        break;
    case 4:
        cs->state = 5;
        break;
    }
    return cs->state;
}
```

This function has to be called at regular intervals within the polling loop to keep the WiFi task progressing. The main program simply has to keep calling pollConnection until it gets a return value of six, indicating that the data is available for processing in the buffer.

This use of a polling function is a general strategy that allows you to hide the fact that callbacks are being used. As far as the main program is concerned all we have is a function that moves the task along each time you call it until the task is complete. Also notice that you can treat this as blocking by simply including a loop that waits until the polling is complete;

```
int state=pollConnection(&cs);
while(cs.state!=6){
        state=pollConnection(&cs);
        sleep_ms(100);
    }
```

When the while loop ends the data is available for processing.

With the polling function and the newConnection function the main program becomes:

```
int main()
{
    stdio_init_all();
    connect();

    struct connectionState cs;
    newConnection(&cs, myBuff);

    ip_addr_t ip;
    IP4_ADDR(&ip, 93, 184, 216, 34);
    cyw43_arch_lwip_begin();
    err_t err = altcp_connect(cs.pcb, &ip, 80, connected);
    cyw43_arch_lwip_end();
    cs.state = 1;
    while (true)
    {
        if (pollConnection(&cs) == 6)
        {
            printf("Buffer= %s\n", cs.myBuff);
            cs.state = 0;
            break;
        }
        sleep_ms(1000);
        printf("LED Flash\n");
    }
    printf("Data Transferred\n");
}
```

The only callbacks that need modifying are `connected`, `poll` and `recv`. The only change to `connected` and `poll` is the need to cast `arg` to a pointer of the correct type:

```
static err_t connected(void *arg, struct altcp_pcb *pcb, err_t err)
{
    struct connectionState *cs = (struct connectionState *)arg;
    cs->state = 2;
    return ERR_OK;
}
err_t poll(void *arg, struct altcp_pcb *pcb)
{
    printf("Connection Closed \n");
    struct connectionState *cs = (struct connectionState *)arg;
    cs->state = 6;
    altcp_close(pcb);
}
```

The `recv` callback needs to be modified so that each time it is called it adds data to the specified buffer rather than overwriting what is already stored there. In this way the buffer builds up the complete data from multiple packets:

```
err_t recv(void *arg, struct altcp_pcb *pcb, struct pbuf *p,
                                             err_t err)
{
    struct connectionState *cs = (struct connectionState *)arg;
    if (p != NULL)
    {
        printf("recv total %d  this buffer %d next %d err %d\n",
                              p->tot_len, p->len, p->next, err);
        if ((p->tot_len) > 2)
        {
            pbuf_copy_partial(p, (cs->myBuff) +
                                    (cs->start), p->tot_len, 0);
            cs->start += p->tot_len;
            cs->myBuff[cs->start] = 0;
            cs->state = 4;
            altcp_recved(pcb, p->tot_len);
        }
        pbuf_free(p);
    }
    else
    {
        printf("Connection Closed\n");
        altcp_close(pcb);
        cs->state = 6;
    }
    return ERR_OK;
}
```

If you make these modifications and run the program you will find that the web page is downloaded as before.

With this change the complete program is:

```c
#include <stdio.h>
#include "pico/stdlib.h"
#include "pico/cyw43_arch.h"
#include "setupWifi.h"
#include "lwip/altcp.h"

#define BUF_SIZE 2048
char myBuff[BUF_SIZE];
char header[] = "GET /index.html HTTP/1.1\r\n
                                HOST:example.com\r\n\r\n";
struct connectionState
{
    int state;
    struct altcp_pcb *pcb;
    char *myBuff;
    int start;
};

err_t sent(void *arg, struct altcp_pcb *pcb, u16_t len)
{
    printf("data sent %d\n", len);
}

err_t recv(void *arg, struct altcp_pcb *pcb,
                                    struct pbuf *p, err_t err)
{
    struct connectionState *cs = (struct connectionState *)arg;
    if (p != NULL)
    {
        printf("recv total %d  this buffer %d next %d err %d\n",
                            p->tot_len, p->len, p->next, err);
        if ((p->tot_len) > 2)
        {
            pbuf_copy_partial(p, (cs->myBuff) +
                                    (cs->start), p->tot_len, 0);
            cs->start += p->tot_len;
            cs->myBuff[cs->start] = 0;
            cs->state = 4;
            altcp_recved(pcb, p->tot_len);
        }
        pbuf_free(p);
    }
```

```
    else
    {
        printf("Connection Closed\n");
        altcp_close(pcb);
        cs->state = 6;
    }
    return ERR_OK;
}

static err_t connected(void *arg, struct altcp_pcb *pcb, err_t err)
{
    struct connectionState *cs = (struct connectionState *)arg;
    cs->state = 2;
    return ERR_OK;
}

err_t poll(void *arg, struct altcp_pcb *pcb)
{
    printf("Connection Closed \n");
    struct connectionState *cs = (struct connectionState *)arg;
    cs->state = 6;
    altcp_close(pcb);
}

void err(void *arg, err_t err)
{
    if (err != ERR_ABRT)
    {
        printf("client_err %d\n", err);
    }
}

err_t newConnection(struct connectionState *cs, char *buf)
{
    cs->state = 0;
    cs->pcb = altcp_new(NULL);
    altcp_recv(cs->pcb, recv);
    altcp_sent(cs->pcb, sent);
    altcp_err(cs->pcb, err);
    altcp_poll(cs->pcb, poll, 10);
    altcp_arg(cs->pcb, cs);
    cs->myBuff = buf;
    cs->start = 0;
    return ERR_OK;
}
```

```c
int pollConnection(struct connectionState *cs)
{
    switch (cs->state)
    {
    case 0:
    case 1:
    case 3:
    case 6:
        break;
    case 2:
        cs->state = 3;
        cyw43_arch_lwip_begin();
        err_t err = altcp_write(cs->pcb, header,
                                        strlen(header), 0);
        err = altcp_output(cs->pcb);
        cyw43_arch_lwip_end();
        break;
    case 4:
        cs->state = 5;
        break;
    }
    return cs->state;
}

int main()
{
    stdio_init_all();
    connect();

    struct connectionState cs;
    newConnection(&cs, myBuff);

    ip_addr_t ip;
    IP4_ADDR(&ip, 93, 184, 216, 34);
    cyw43_arch_lwip_begin();
    err_t err = altcp_connect(cs.pcb, &ip, 80, connected);
    cyw43_arch_lwip_end();
    cs.state = 1;
    while (true)
    {
        if (pollConnection(&cs) == 6)
        {
            printf("Buffer= %s\n", cs.myBuff);
            cs.state = 0;
            break;
        }
        sleep_ms(1000);
        printf("LED Flash\n");
    }
    printf("Data Transferred\n");
}
```

As already mentioned, the pollConnection function has to be called to keep the connection making progress. When cs.state is 6 the data is available in the buffer. This approach is related to the idea of using a promise. When pollConnection returns 6 the promise has resolved and the data is ready. To make this more like a promise you would have to hide the polling loop and use a dispatch queue approach.

Although it is easy to use the polling function to block the main program, you can easily convert the polling function itself into a blocking function:

```
int waitForConnection(struct connectionState *cs){
    int state=pollConnection(cs);
    while(cs->state!=0){
        state=pollConnection(cs);
        sleep_ms(100);
    }
    return cs->state;
}
```

This function now blocks until the request has been completed, the connection has been closed and the data is ready to be processed. Notice that this has the disadvantage of not allowing anything else to happen while the data is being downloaded.

The only difference between blocking and non-blocking in this context is where the polling loop is. For a blocking function the polling loop is internal whereas for a non-blocking loop the function is called from an external loop.

General Request Function

The HTTP interaction is very standard and it is easy to keep moving up one level of abstraction in its implementation. For example, often all you want to do is make an HTTP request to a particular IP address and port. This can be wrapped up in a single non-blocking request function.

A non-blocking request function needs to share more state with the polling function. In particular, it has to provide access to the cs struct and to the data to be sent to the server after the connection has been made. The simplest way to do this is to extend the definition of the struct and create it on the heap. Of course, this means we have to remember to free the memory used.

The new struct is:

```
struct connectionState
{
    int state;
    struct altcp_pcb *pcb;
    char *sendData;
    char *recvData;
    int start;
};
```

The `sendData` parameter is a string that is sent to the server and the `recvData` is a buffer ready to receive the data.

We need a `newConnection` function to create the struct and return it:

```
struct connectionState *newConnection(char *sendData,
                                      char *recvData)
{
  struct connectionState *cs = (struct connectionState *)
                  malloc(sizeof(struct connectionState));
  cs->state = 0;
  cs->pcb = altcp_new(NULL);
  altcp_recv(cs->pcb, recv);
  altcp_sent(cs->pcb, sent);
  altcp_err(cs->pcb, err);
  altcp_poll(cs->pcb, poll, 10);
  altcp_arg(cs->pcb, cs);
  cs->sendData = sendData;
  cs->recvData = recvData;
  cs->start = 0;
  return cs;
}
```

The general `doRequest` function is:

```
struct connectionState *doRequest(ip_addr_t *ip, char *host,
     u16_t port, char *request, char *file,
                  char *sendData, char *recvData)
{
  char headerTemplate[] = "%s %s HTTP/1.1\r\n
                           HOST:%s:%d\r\n
                           Connection: close\r\n
                           Content-length: %d\r\n\r\n\r\n%s";
  int len = snprintf(NULL, 0, headerTemplate, request,
              file, host, port, strlen(sendData), sendData);
  char *requestData = malloc(len + 1);
  snprintf(requestData, len + 1, headerTemplate, request,
              file, host, port, strlen(sendData), sendData);
  struct connectionState *cs = newConnection(requestData,
                                             recvData);
  cyw43_arch_lwip_begin();
  err_t err = altcp_connect(cs->pcb, ip, port, connected);
  cyw43_arch_lwip_end();
  cs->state = 1;
  return cs;
}
```

This starts off by building a set of request headers based on the parameters supplied. The caller has to provided the `ip` address and `port` to connect to and the `host` name. The `request` parameter has to be a string like "GET" or "PUT", the `file` gives the file involved in the transaction. Notice that `recvData` has to be large enough to store the data sent by the server – no checks are made to ensure that this is the case. The snprintf function is used to construct the headers. Notice the use of snprintf(NULL,0,... to find the length of the constructed string.

Once the headers are constructed the PCB is created and initialized and then we go through the usual states to actually transfer the data between the server and the client. The pollRequest function is:

```
int pollRequest(struct connectionState **pcs)
{
 if(*pcs==NULL) return 0;
 struct connectionState *cs=*pcs;
 switch (cs->state)
 {
   case 0:
   case 1:
   case 3:
         break;

   case 2:
         cs->state = 3;
         cyw43_arch_lwip_begin();
         err_t err = altcp_write(cs->pcb, cs→sendData,
                            strlen(cs->sendData), 0);
         err = altcp_output(cs->pcb);
         cyw43_arch_lwip_end();
         break;
   case 4:
         cs->state = 5;
         break;
   case 6:
         cyw43_arch_lwip_begin();
         altcp_close(cs->pcb);
         cyw43_arch_lwip_end();
         free(cs);
         *pcs = NULL;
         return 0;
 }
   return cs->state;
}
```

To make managing the struct allocated on the heap easier we pass a pointer to a pointer to the struct so we can set cs to NULL in the main program. Notice that now we have to close the PCB and free the cs struct. By setting the cs pointer to NULL we can avoid freeing it multiple times and lock the state to be 0 i.e. not connected. That is if the polling function is passed a NULL pointer to the struct then state has to 0. We also need to take the close action out of the callbacks to avoid duplication.

You can convert this function into a library by creating a header and a C file, but a simpler solution while developing a program is to place the function and everything it uses into a header file. Create a file called `request.h` and enter:

```c
struct connectionState
{
    int state;
    struct altcp_pcb *pcb;
    char *sendData;
    char *recvData;
    int start;
};

err_t sent(void *arg, struct altcp_pcb *pcb, u16_t len)
{
    printf("data sent %d\n", len);
}

err_t recv(void *arg, struct altcp_pcb *pcb,
                                    struct pbuf *p, err_t err)
{
    struct connectionState *cs = (struct connectionState *)arg;
    if (p != NULL)
    {
        printf("recv total %d  this buffer %d next %d err %d\n",
                            p->tot_len, p->len, p->next, err);
        if ((p->tot_len) > 2)
        {
            pbuf_copy_partial(p, (cs->recvData) +
                                    (cs->start), p->tot_len, 0);
            cs->start += p->tot_len;
            cs->recvData[cs->start] = 0;
            cs->state = 4;
            altcp_recved(pcb, p->tot_len);
        }
        pbuf_free(p);
    }
    else
    {
        cs->state = 6;
    }
    return ERR_OK;
}

static err_t connected(void *arg, struct altcp_pcb *pcb, err_t err)
{
    struct connectionState *cs = (struct connectionState *)arg;
    cs->state = 2;
    return ERR_OK;
}
```

```c
err_t poll(void *arg, struct altcp_pcb *pcb)
{
    printf("Connection Closed \n");
    struct connectionState *cs = (struct connectionState *)arg;
    cs->state = 6;
}
void err(void *arg, err_t err)
{
    if (err != ERR_ABRT)
    {
        printf("client_err %d\n", err);
    }
}
struct connectionState *newConnection(char *sendData,
                                                char *recvData)
{
    struct connectionState *cs = (struct connectionState *)
                      malloc(sizeof(struct connectionState));
    cs->state = 0;
    cs->pcb = altcp_new(NULL);
    altcp_recv(cs->pcb, recv);
    altcp_sent(cs->pcb, sent);
    altcp_err(cs->pcb, err);
    altcp_poll(cs->pcb, poll, 10);
    altcp_arg(cs->pcb, cs);
    cs->sendData = sendData;
    cs->recvData = recvData;
    cs->start = 0;
    return cs;
}
struct connectionState *doRequest(ip_addr_t *ip, char *host,
        u16_t port, char *request, char *file,
                            char *sendData, char *recvData)
{
    char headerTemplate[] = "%s %s HTTP/1.1\r\n
                                HOST:%s:%d\r\n
                                Connection: close\r\n
                                Content-length: %d\r\n\r\n%s";
    int len = snprintf(NULL, 0, headerTemplate, request,
                  file, host, port, strlen(sendData), sendData);
    char *requestData = malloc(len + 1);
    snprintf(requestData, len + 1, headerTemplate,
          request, file, host, port, strlen(sendData), sendData);
    struct connectionState *cs = newConnection(requestData,
                                                recvData);
    cyw43_arch_lwip_begin();
    err_t err = altcp_connect(cs->pcb, ip, port, connected);
    cyw43_arch_lwip_end();
    cs->state = 1;
    return cs;
}
```

```c
int pollRequest(struct connectionState **pcs)
{
    if(*pcs==NULL) return 0;
    struct connectionState *cs=*pcs;
    switch (cs->state)
    {
    case 0:
    case 1:
    case 3:
        break;

    case 2:
        cs->state = 3;
        cyw43_arch_lwip_begin();
        err_t err = altcp_write(cs->pcb, cs->sendData,
                                    strlen(cs->sendData), 0);
        err = altcp_output(cs->pcb);
        cyw43_arch_lwip_end();
        break;
    case 4:
        cs->state = 5;
        break;
    case 6:
        cyw43_arch_lwip_begin();
        altcp_close(cs->pcb);
        cyw43_arch_lwip_end();
        free(cs);
        *pcs = NULL;
        return 0;
    }
    return cs->state;
}
```

With this header file we can now write a main program to perform a GET and a PUT:

```c
#include <stdio.h>
#include "pico/stdlib.h"
#include "pico/cyw43_arch.h"

#include "lwip/altcp.h"
#include "setupWifi.h"
#include "request.h"
#define BUF_SIZE 2048
char myBuff[BUF_SIZE];

int main()
{
    stdio_init_all();
    connect();

    ip_addr_t ip;
    IP4_ADDR(&ip, 93, 184, 216, 34);
    struct connectionState *cs = doRequest(&ip, "example.com", 80,
                                    "GET", "/", NULL, myBuff);
    while (pollRequest(&cs))
    {
        sleep_ms(100);
    }
    printf("Buffer= %s\n", myBuff);

    IP4_ADDR(&ip, 192, 168, 11, 101);
    cs = doRequest(&ip, "192.168.11.101", 8080,
                        "PUT", "/", "Hello PUT world", myBuff);
    while (pollRequest(&cs))
    {
        sleep_ms(100);
    }
    printf("Buffer= %s\n", myBuff);
    printf("Data Transferred\n");
}
```

Of course, the idea is that you would do useful work in the polling loops rather than just waiting for the data to be available. Notice that you have to pass the address of cs to the polling loop and it is set to NULL when the connection is closed and after this pollRequest returns 0 whenever it is called.

Using this approach you can also make simultaneous requests:

```
int main()
{
    stdio_init_all();
    connect();

    ip_addr_t ip;
    IP4_ADDR(&ip, 93, 184, 216, 34);
    struct connectionState *cs1 = doRequest(&ip, "example.com", 80,
                                    "GET", "/", NULL, myBuff1);
    IP4_ADDR(&ip, 192, 168, 11, 101);
    struct connectionState *cs2 = doRequest(&ip, "192.168.11.101",
                        8080, "PUT", "/", "Hello PUT world", myBuff2);

    while (pollRequest(&cs1) + pollRequest(&cs2))
    {
        sleep_ms(100);
    }
    printf("Both complete\n");
    printf("Buffer 1 = \n%s\n\n", myBuff1);
    printf("Buffer 2 = \n%s\n\n", myBuff2);

    printf("Data Transferred\n");
    cyw43_arch_deinit();
    return 0;
}
```

Notice that we need to use the addition operator in the while rather than a logical operator. This is because logical operators are lazy evaluated and if the first polling function returns non-zero the second polling function isn't called. Forming the sum of the results means you evaluate both functions each time through the loop. The GET downloaded the example.com page and the PUT sends some data to the custom server introduced in Chapter 2.

You will find a full listing of the request header file and the main program on the book's web page at I/O Press.

A Temperature Sensor Client

While HTTP was invented to allow the transport of HTML pages, it can be used to transfer any data between the client and the server.

It is important to understand what the distinction is between the client and the server. In this case the client initiates the connection and the server accepts the connection. The connection once established is two-way – the client can send data to the server and vice versa. This said, HTTP is most commonly used to send data from the server to the client in the form of web pages.

The standard approach to implementing a sensor device that makes its readings available to other devices is to implement a web server or a custom protocol that allows other devices to connect. A simpler solution is to implement an HTTP client and allow the sensor device to send data to a server which other devices can then connect to as required. All we have to do is take a reading every so often, convert the floating-point value to a byte object and send it to the server using a PUT with a non-blocking request:

```c
#include <stdio.h>
#include "pico/stdlib.h"
#include "pico/cyw43_arch.h"
#include "setupWifi.h"
#include "lwip/altcp.h"
#include "request.h"
#define BUF_SIZE 4096
char myBuff1[BUF_SIZE];
int readTemp()
{
    return 33;
}
int main()
{
    char ssid[] = "laribina";
    char pass[] = "hawkhawk";
    uint32_t country = CYW43_COUNTRY_UK;
    uint32_t auth = CYW43_AUTH_WPA2_MIXED_PSK;
    stdio_init_all();
    setup(country, ssid, pass, auth, "MyPicoW", NULL, NULL, NULL);
    ip_addr_t ip;
    IP4_ADDR(&ip, 192, 168, 11, 101);

    while (true)
    {
        int t = readTemp();
        int len = snprintf(NULL, 0, "%d", t);
        char *requestData = malloc(len + 1);
        snprintf(requestData, len + 1, "%d", t);
        printf("%s\n",requestData);
        struct connectionState *cs1 = doRequest(&ip,
                          "192.168.11.101", 8080,
                          "PUT", "/", requestData, myBuff1);
        while (pollRequest(&cs1) )
        {
            sleep_ms(200);
        }
        printf("%s\n",myBuff1);
        sleep_ms(5000);
    }
    return 0;
}
```

Instead of complicating the example with code to implement a sensor reading, the readTemp function simply returns a fixed value. This is then converted into a string and PUT to the server. The 200ms polling loop could be absorbed into the 5000ms polling loop using a simple if test on the number of times through the loop. The idea is that other tasks could be undertaken during the polling loop.

A suitable custom server in Python is:

```python
from http.server import HTTPServer, BaseHTTPRequestHandler
from io import BytesIO

class SimpleHTTPRequestHandler(BaseHTTPRequestHandler):

    def log_message(self,*args, **kwargs):
        pass

    def do_PUT(self):
        content_length = int(self.headers['Content-Length'])
        body = self.rfile.read(content_length)
        bodyString= body.decode(encoding="utf-8")
        temp=float(bodyString)
        print(temp)
        self.send_response(200)
        self.end_headers()

httpd = HTTPServer(('', 8080), SimpleHTTPRequestHandler)
httpd.serve_forever()
```

This simply displays the temperature as it is received. Of course you could send more data and use encodings such as XML or JSON.

The point of this example is to indicate that an IoT (Internet of Things) device doesn't have to be a server to make data available to the outside world. A single server can be used to aggregate and redistribute data with the IoT devices acting as clients.

A Binary Client

It is often thought that HTTP is a text based protocol. This is true as far as the headers go but the payload can be binary – or octets in the jargon of IP. Creating a PUT request client is fairly easy as all we really have to do is modify our existing request handler to cope with sending fixed length buffers rather than strings. This is easier if we introduce a second request function which sends a binary buffer:

```
struct connectionState *doRequestBinary(ip_addr_t *ip, char *host,
          u16_t port, char *request, char *file,
                      char *sendData,int bytes, char *recvData)
{

    char headerTemplate[] = "%s %s HTTP/1.1\r\n
                             HOST:%s:%d\r\n
                             Connection: close\r\n
                             Content-length: %d\r\n\r\n";
    int len = snprintf(NULL, 0, headerTemplate, request,
                                  file, host, port, bytes);
    char *requestData = malloc(len + bytes+1);
    snprintf(requestData, len+1, headerTemplate,
                        request, file, host, port, bytes);
    memcpy(requestData+len,sendData,bytes);

    struct connectionState *cs = newConnection(requestData,len +
                                               bytes ,recvData);
    cyw43_arch_lwip_begin();
    err_t err = altcp_connect(cs->pcb, ip, port, connected);
    cyw43_arch_lwip_end();
    cs->state = 1;
    return cs;
}
```

You can see that we now have to pass the length of the sendData buffer because it cannot be worked out by the position of a zero byte which ends a string. We also cannot use string handling functions to build the entire request data. The headers, however, can be constructed using the same technique based on snprint. After this we need to copy the binary data in sendData into the correct position in the requestData buffer using memcpy.

Of course, we also need to modify the original doRequest() to use the length of the string:

```
struct connectionState *cs = newConnection(requestData,
                                    strlen(requestData),recvData);
```

We also need to modify the connectionState struct to hold the size of the sendData buffer:

```
struct connectionState
{
    int state;
    struct altcp_pcb *pcb;
    char *sendData;
    int bytes;
    char *recvData;
    int start;
};
```

and change its initialization:

```
struct connectionState *newConnection(char *sendData, int bytes,
char *recvData)
{
    struct connectionState *cs = (struct connectionState *)
                      malloc(sizeof(struct connectionState));
    cs->state = 0;
    cs->pcb = altcp_new(NULL);
    altcp_recv(cs->pcb, recv);
    altcp_sent(cs->pcb, sent);
    altcp_err(cs->pcb, err);
    altcp_poll(cs->pcb, poll, 10);
    altcp_arg(cs->pcb, cs);
    cs->sendData = sendData;
    cs->bytes=bytes;
    cs->recvData = recvData;
    cs->start = 0;
    return cs;
}
```

We also need to modify the poll request for state==2 to make it send the correct number of bytes:

```
int pollRequest(struct connectionState *cs)
{
    if (cs == NULL)
        return 0;
    if (cs->state == 2)
    {
        cs->state = 3;
        cyw43_arch_lwip_begin();
        err_t err = altcp_write(cs->pcb, cs->sendData,
                                        cs->bytes, 0);
        err = altcp_output(cs->pcb);
        cyw43_arch_lwip_end();
    }
```

73

It should also be obvious that you don't actually need the string based doRequest if you have the doRequestBinary function as all you need to do is pass in the length of the string but it is useful if you need to customize the headers sent in each case.

A main program using this is fairly obvious – the only change being the need to set the size of the buffer:

```
int main()
{
    stdio_init_all();
    connect();
    char randdata[500];

    ip_addr_t ip;
    IP4_ADDR(&ip, 192, 168, 11, 101);

    for (int p = 0; p < 500; p++)
    {
        randdata[p] = (uint8_t)rand();
    }
    struct connectionState *cs1 = doRequestBinary(&ip,
                "192.168.11.101", 8080,
                        "PUT", "/", randdata,500, myBuff);

    while (pollRequest(cs1))
    {
        sleep_ms(200);
    }
    printf("%s\n", myBuff);
    return 0;
}
```

This program sends 500 bytes of random binary data to the server. You can see the full listing for this and the latest version of request.h on the book's page at www.iopress.info.

We can also modify the custom Python server given earlier so that it saves the binary data it receives in a file:

```python
from http.server import HTTPServer, BaseHTTPRequestHandler
from io import BytesIO

class SimpleHTTPRequestHandler(BaseHTTPRequestHandler):

    def log_message(self,*args, **kwargs):
        pass

    def do_PUT(self):
        content_length = int(self.headers['Content-Length'])
        body = self.rfile.read(content_length)
        print(content_length)
        with open("data.bin",mode="wb") as f:
            f.write(body)
        self.send_response(200)
        self.end_headers()
        response = BytesIO()
        response.write(b'Received:' )
        self.wfile.write(response.getvalue())

httpd = HTTPServer(('', 8080), SimpleHTTPRequestHandler)
httpd.serve_forever()
```

You can, of course arrange to save or use the binary data in any way you want. Some servers will expect additional headers for binary data, but mostly they aren't necessary. For example:

```
Content-Type: application/octet-stream
```

is a header that tells the server that the payload is raw binary.

DNS

So far we have used the IP address of the server that we want to connect to but lwIP has a DNS module that allows you to make basic DNS queries. What is more, this module is integrated with the WiFi driver so that it is automatically enabled and initialized to any DNS servers supplied by DHCP. What this means is that, in most cases, all we have to do to look up a URL and find its IP address is to use:

```
err_t dns_gethostbyname(const char *hostname, ip_addr_t *addr,
                 dns_found_callback found, void *callback_arg)
```

The first parameter is the host name of the server you want to lookup. The second is a pointer to an ip_addr_t struct ready to receive the IP address of the host. The third parameter is a callback that is used to deliver the IP address after a full DNS lookup and the final parameter is a custom argument to be passed to the callback.

You also need to add:

```
#include "lwip/dns.h"
```

This is a superficially simple API function, but in fact it is quite complicated. The complication stems from the fact that the DNS module keeps a list of host names that have already been looked up and so there are two distinct ways that an IP address can be delivered. If the IP address is already in the list then the function copies it into the addr parameter and returns with ERR_OK. If the IP address isn't in the list the function initiates a DNS lookup and returns immediately with ERR_INPROGRESS. Of course, in this case the IP address isn't returned in addr. Instead the found callback is called with the IP address when it is available. The signature of the callback is:

```
void *dns_found_callback(const char *name,
                 const ip_addr_t *ipaddr, void *callback_arg)
```

The name is the host name you looked up, ipaddr is a pointer to the IP address it found and arg is the custom argument. Notice the ipaddr is not the same struct as the one used in the original callback to a struct in the internal list of IP address. If the IP address cannot be found ipaddr is set to NULL.

This all sounds reasonable, but it complicates matters as there are not only two times that the IP address can be returned, but two distinct ways. The obvious solution to the problem is arrange things so that the callback can be called if the IP address is already available. Something like:

```
ip_addr_t ipResult;
cyw43_arch_lwip_begin();
err_t err = dns_gethostbyname(URL, &ipResult, dns_found, NULL);
cyw43_arch_lwip_end();
if (err == ERR_OK)
{
        dns_found(URL, &ipResult, NULL);
}
```

A slightly more sophisticated approach is to implement a non-blocking call which hides the callback. The basic idea is to return a struct which eventually resolves to a value with the help of the callback. This is similar, but much simpler, to using a promise or a future in other languages. The advantage is that you can choose to block or poll on the status of the struct.

The getIP function below simply passes the pointer to the ip_addr_t struct that the main program has created to the callback. The main program has to ensure that the struct has been zeroed as this is used to test for a valid IP. If the call finds the IP address in the cache then ipResult already has a valid IP address stored in it and the callback is never called.

```
err_t getIP(char *URL, ip_addr_t *ipResult)
{
    cyw43_arch_lwip_begin();
    err_t err = dns_gethostbyname(URL, ipResult,
                                    dns_found, ipResult);
    cyw43_arch_lwip_end();
    return err;
}
```

If the IP address isn't in the cache then the callback is eventually called:

```
void dns_found(const char *name, const ip_addr_t *ip, void *arg)
{
    ip_addr_t *ipResult = (ip_addr_t *)arg;
    if (ip)
    {
        ip4_addr_copy(*ipResult, *ip);
    }
    else
    {
        ip4_addr_set_loopback(ipResult);
    }
    return;
}
```

This checks to see if ip is non-NULL and if it is then it copies the result to the ip_addr_t struct that was originally passed in to getIP. If it is NULL then the address cannot be found and it sets the passed in the struct ipResult to the loopback address which is safe to use as an "error" indicator as a DNS lookup should never produce a loopback address.

To use this from a main program you would use something like:

```
ip_addr_t ip;
ip4_addr_set_zero(&ip);
getIP("example.com", &ip);
while (!ip_addr_get_ip4_u32(&ip))
{
    sleep_ms(100);
};
if(ip4_addr_isloopback(&ip) ){
    printf("address not found");
}
```

Notice that you have to zero the `ip` struct each time otherwise the polling loop would end prematurely. Of course, in a real application that polling loop might well do some useful work while waiting for the IP address. You should also add a test for an initial error.

You can use these functions and this polling loop to look up any IP address you need to use. In the rest of the examples an explicit IP address is used for simplicity.

You can find out what DNS servers are being used via:

```
const ip_addr_t *dns_getserver(u8_t numdns)
```

which returns the IP address of the DNS server selected. There are a maximum of two servers set by default. For example, to see the IP of the first server:

```
const ip_addr_t *ipDNS=dns_getserver(0) ;
printf("%s\n", ipaddr_ntoa(ipDNS));
```

Any uninitialized servers return `0.0.0.0`.. You can also set a server using:

```
void dns_setserver(u8_t numdns, const ip_addr_t *dnsserver)
```

You have to ensure that `numdns<DNS_MAX_SERVERS`, which is usually set to two in the configuration file.

Summary

- The RAW API is based on using callbacks to deal with asynchronous actions rather than more modern approaches such as promises or async/await.

- The problem with callbacks is that they distort the natural flow of control and it is difficult to know how to organize a program around their use.

- One easy solution is to maintain a state variable that can be updated by the callbacks and examined by the main program to determine what to do next.

- Usually the state variable has to record multiple aspects of the current state and therefore it is usually better to use a struct.

- The state struct can be passed to all of the callbacks using the default arg parameter that they all support, thus avoiding the need to use global variables.

- As a further abstraction on the use of state, we can create a polling function that the main program can call to move the state on and to discover when the process is complete.

- Using this approach it is easy to create a general HTTP request function that can be used for GET, PUT or any of of the requests.

- It is tempting to think that when an IoT device needs to send data it should be implemented as a server, but there are lots of advantages in implementing it as a client and using PUT or POST.

- Although HTTP is generally thought of as a text-oriented protocol, it can be used to send binary data.

- The lwIP library provides the ability to do DNS lookups, but this can be tricky because it also caches the results of previous lookups and delivers them in a different way.

Chapter 4

SSL/TLS and HTTPS

HTTP using TCP/IP is a simple and relatively efficient way to transport data, but it isn't secure. Today many web servers will only deliver data if it is protected by encryption and identity confirmation using HTTPS. This, and the general concern for security, causes problems for IoT programmers. Security, and encryption in particular, are not cheap in terms of the resources needed to implement them, but if you are planning to make your code available to the wider world you really don't have a choice but to implement security. There are many ways of doing this but the best advice is, if possible, don't do it from scratch. If you are not a security expert you are likely to get it wrong and make all of the effort you put into building something "secure" a waste of time. Users also like to know that your application is secure by recognizing well known standards. In short, there is a lot of pressure to use security standards even if they might be more than is actually required for an IoT device.

What this means in practice is that you most likely need to support HTTPS for web-based interactions and SSL/TLS (Secure Sockets Layer/Transport Layer Security), which is the basis of HTTPS, for other interactions. Fortunately, lwIP has a degree of integration with a very standard SSL/TLS library, mbedTLS.

In this chapter we look at how to use mbedTLS to create an HTTPS client, but this is just a step in using mbedTLS to implement a range of secure data transfers.

Public Key Certificates

The basis of modern security is Public Key Infrastructure, PKI. This in turn is based on the use of public key, or asymmetrical, cryptography. The simplest approach to cryptography is to use the same key for encryption as decryption. In this case, the key is private and has to be known to both the sender and the receiver and has to be kept secret from everyone else. This creates the problem of "key exchange". How can you get a key securely from the sender to the receiver of the data. In transit the key is vulnerable.

Public key cryptography is amazing because it works with two keys – a public key that anyone can know and use to encrypt a message and a private key that only the receiver knows and can be used to decrypt the message. This is asymmetrical cryptography because different keys are used for encryption and decryption. Its big advantage is that it removes the need to exchange keys. Its big disadvantage is that it is very slow. Because it is so slow and inefficient public key cryptography is used to exchange symmetric keys. That is, most of the time you are using symmetric key cryptography with keys provided by public key cryptography. Keys are generally stored in a special format that associates the keys with an identity – a certificate.

What happens is that, when a client connects to a server, the private and public keys are used to create a shared encryption key which is then used for all further communication. There are two general situations. If the server has a certificate but the client doesn't then the client generates a random number and uses the server's public key to securely send this to the server. Of course, as only the server has the private key only the server can decrypt the message and so the client and the server now have a shared secret that they can use to generate a symmetric key. The second situation is where both parties have a certificate and in this case the private and public keys available at each end of the connection are used to transport a random number to act as a shared secret.

What this means in practice is that a client doesn't need a certificate to establish secure communication. A client only needs a certificate if it needs to prove its identity. What is more, a client IoT device is less secure with a certificate that contains a private key as this has to be stored in the device and most don't have the necessary hardware to stop someone from connecting to the device and reading the key. Servers can keep their private keys secure because they are physically secure and protecting the key is a matter of software security. For most IoT devices no amount of software security can keep the key safe from a physical attack.

It is also important to know that key exchange can occur more than once in the lifetime of a connection to ensure the maximum security. The actual symmetric key encryption algorithm that is used can also be negotiated between the client and server. This all makes the connection more complicated.

Encryption solves the privacy issue, but it doesn't solve the identity problem. How does the client know that the server it is connecting to is the real server and not an impostor? This is where digital certificates come into the picture. At the simplest level, a certificate is simply a container for a pair of public and private keys. More commonly the certificate only contains the public key – the private key being stored in a separate key file – this allows the certificate to be shared. Certificates also contain other information about the entity that the certificate is issued to, such as name, address, domain name and so on. Obtaining a certificate is one way for a client to gain information about a server including its public key which allows key exchange to take place.

Certificates are also digitally signed to indicate their validity. Of course, how much trust you can put in the certificate depends on who signed it. You can easily create a certificate that you also sign – a self-signed certificate - and while this is useful as a way to supply a public key, it does nothing to prove that you are who you claim to be. To be convincing evidence of identity a certificate has to be digitally signed by one of a number of well-known certificate-issuing authorities. The certificate-issuing authority will make checks and ask for documentation that proves who you are and for this it makes a charge.

How can you know that a certificate-issuing authority is authentic? It is usually the case that the certificate-issuing authority has a certificate that proves who they are, signed by another, higher, authority. This leads to the idea of a chain of certificates which ultimately end in a signature from a trusted final authority with a certificate that is installed in most browsers and used to give the final verdict on the validity of a certificate. Following a certificate chain and validating an identity is time-consuming and resource heavy.

At the time of writing, the Pico uses certificates for encryption, but doesn't validate certificates to confirm identities.

SSL and TLS

A very common use of certificates is in TLS, Transport Security Layer. This is used in HTTPS to transport data between client and server, but it is also used in email and other types of server. TLS evolved out of SSL, Secure Sockets Layer which is still used to refer to it. SSL was designed to be used to convert a standard non-encrypted socket-based connection to an encrypted socket-based connection with minimal change to the program. As the Pico, without the help of Free RTOS, doesn't make use of lwIP's socket API you might think that SSL wasn't relevant, but TLS/SSL can convert a callback-based program into an encrypted connection with very little extra work, as long as you have used the ALTCP introduced in Chapter 2, which provides the same versatility as sockets.

That is:

- TLS/SSL is a way to add encryption and authentication to existing protocols.
- SSL is now obsolete but you will still find that TLS libraries and facilities have SSL in their name even though they support TLS, e.g. the OPENSSL library.
- TLS is generally added to a socket-based implementation of a protocol and, on the Pico, lwIP doesn't support sockets unless you also use Free RTOS.
- As long as you have used ALTCP to implement your program, you can add TLS with very few changes.

There have been a number of revisions of the TLS/SSL protocol over time. The first three versions were SSL 1 to 3 and these are all deprecated. TLS 1.0 was issued in 1999 and deprecated in 2021. TLS 1.1 was also deprecated in 2021. The two supported versions are TLS 1.2, introduced in 2008, and TLS 1.3, introduced in 2018.

At the time of writing TLS 1.2 is supported by 99% of all servers and TLS 1.3 by 54.2%. A server can support multiple versions of TLS and roughly 40% still support TLS 1.0 and 1.1.

All latest web browsers support TLS 1.0, 1.1 and 1.2 by default. TLS 1.3 is thought to be secure in all its possible configurations, but TLS 1.2 has vulnerabilities if you select a weak configuration. Currently the mbedTLS library that the Pico uses supports TLS 1.2.

Every TLS connection starts out unencrypted. The client then requests that the server sets up a TLS connection. Usually this happens if the client attempts to connect using port 443, but it can also use a protocol-specific STARTTLS request to the server; this is often used with email servers.

The next step is that a handshaking procedure starts using public keys. The handshake establishes what encryption and hash methods the client and server support. The server picks a method that they both support. Next the server sends the client its certificate and the client checks it for validity. The client can also provide a certificate to the server for it to check. Finally a shared secret is constructed by the client and passed to the server.

From this point on everything is encrypted using the agreed method and key. The higher-level protocol, HTTPS in this case, submits its data packets to be transferred and they are automatically encrypted on transmission and decrypted on reception. In this way the program can work as if encryption wasn't being used.

In practice, the server and client often have to have more than one attempt at making the connection work and this can result in empty packets being transmitted and received. HTTPS can be messy.

ALTCP_TLS and mbedTLS

As we already know, the Pico SDK uses lwIP to implement network functions. As long as you have used the altcp module then it is very easy to change the way that the network functions run at run time. The idea is that you can provide a custom module that maps standard functions like altcp_write to a custom implementation. This is a very general method of adding a feature to an existing TCP program.

To make TLS easy to use, lwIP provides an application module, altcp_tls which maps the standard network functions to TLS functions. To make use of this module all you have to do is include altcp_tls.h and set LWIP_ALTCP_TLS to 1 in the lwipopts.h file. However, the altcp_tls module doesn't actually do any cryptography. Instead it passes all of the cryptography tasks on to the mbedtls library.

The mbedtls library is a lightweight cryptographic library aimed at hardware with limited memory and processor power. To make everything work you also need to compile mbedtls and allow altcp_tls to make use of it. This sounds easy, but there are a great many options and customizations needed to make it work as the mbedtls library isn't targeted at any particular hardware.

To customize mbedtls you need to add defines to an additional configuration file, mbedtls_config.h, which is stored in your project folder. The big problem with this configuration file is the huge number of options and the lack of guidance on how to use them. What is worse is that many of the options have to be selected to make anything work at all and options are interlinked and depend on one another. All this makes getting started with mbedtls difficult.

You can include the full mbedtls library in your program using:

target_link_libraries(. . . pico_mbedtls)

i.e. by adding pico_mbedtls to the list of target_link_libraries.

A Simple TLS Client

A good starting point in getting to grips with `mbedtls` is to convert the simplest HTTP client program given in Chapter 2 to HTTPS. The simplicity of this program lets you see where the changes have to be made.

What might surprise you is how easy the conversion to HTTPS is. All you have to do to the main program is add:

```
#include "lwip/altcp_tls.h"
```

and replace the line which constructs the standard TCP PCB:

```
struct altcp_pcb *pcb = altcp_new(NULL);
```

by:

```
struct altcp_tls_config *tls_config =
                        altcp_tls_create_config_client(NULL, 0);
struct altcp_pcb *pcb = altcp_tls_new(tls_config, IPADDR_TYPE_ANY);
```

The `altcp_tls_create_config_client` creates an additional struct to be added to the usual PCB. Usually the first parameter passed is the certificate and the second its length. In this case the client doesn't need a certificate so `NULL` and `0` are appropriate arguments. Once the `config` has been created we can create the extended PCB which includes the details of the TSL connection.

The only other instruction the program needs is to tell the server which certificate it should use:

```
mbedtls_ssl_set_hostname(altcp_tls_context(pcb), "example.com");
```

A single server at a given IP address may be hosting more than one HTTPS site, each with its own certificate. We have to tell the server which website we want to allow it to use the correct certificate.

We also have to change the port being used for the connection:

```
err_t err = altcp_connect(pcb, &ip, 443, connected);
```

With these changes and additions the program will just work as before, but with an HTTPS connection. However, as the program stands it will not compile because we need to make changes to the configuration files. We need to add:

```
#undef TCP_WND
#define TCP_WND  16384

#define LWIP_ALTCP              1
#define LWIP_ALTCP_TLS          1
#define LWIP_ALTCP_TLS_MBEDTLS  1

#define LWIP_DEBUG 1
#define ALTCP_MBEDTLS_DEBUG  LWIP_DBG_ON
#endif /* __LWIPOPTS_H__ */
```

to the end of the usual `lwipopts.h` (the one obtained from `pico/pico-examples/pico_w/lwipopts_examples_common.h`).

The `TCP_WND` needs to be increased because TLS is more demanding. The others enable `altcp`, `altcp_tls` and `mbedtls` as part of the build.

As already mentioned, when using `mbedtls` we also need a new configuration file, `mbedtls_config.h`. This one overrides the default configuration file and you need to set a number of configuration features to make `mbedtls` work at all. There are a huge number of parameters you can change and they are poorly documented and difficult to understand by anyone who isn't an expert in encryption methods. As the whole point of using an encryption library is to avoid having to be an expert this is disappointing. However, it is possible to make sense of the different aspects of configuration. Rather than simply presenting a standard configuration file, we can construct a minimal configuration file and explain what the defines are actually doing.

The mbedtls library is mostly hardware-independent and will run on almost anything with few changes. The only hardware-specific configurations we need are:

```
//Hardware config
#define MBEDTLS_NO_PLATFORM_ENTROPY
#define MBEDTLS_ENTROPY_HARDWARE_ALT
#define MBEDTLS_HAVE_TIME
```

This first tells mbedtls that the Pico doesn't have a source of entropy because it isn't running an operating system. The second promises to provide a function that will return random data, i.e. entropy and the final one states the Pico supports `time.h`.

The source of randomness is in the form of a function:

```
int mbedtls_hardware_poll(void *data, unsigned char *output,
                          size_t len, size_t *olen)
```

This is supplied for us in the file:

`pico/pico-sdk/src/rp2_common/pico_mbedtls/pico_mbedtls.c`

This makes use of the new random functions added to Version 1.5 of the SDK, see the next chapter for more information.

After these three defines, the rest of the configuration file is concerned with which cryptographic methods you want to support. The problem here is trying to work out what to include and what to leave out. If you recall, a TLS connection involves a negotiation step which determines what key exchange protocol to use and what symmetric encryption method to use. The point is that you don't need to support all of the possible methods, but if you don't there will be the occasional connections that cannot be made.

So what key exchange and encryption methods should you support?

Although it is generally accepted that DHE_RSA is more secure, nearly every site supports RSA key exchange so this is what we will use for this first example. Most sites also support AES CCM or AES CBC as an encryption method.

Putting this together with the hardware requirements in a very simple mbedtls_config.h file:

```
//Hardware config
#define MBEDTLS_NO_PLATFORM_ENTROPY
#define MBEDTLS_ENTROPY_HARDWARE_ALT
#define MBEDTLS_HAVE_TIME

//error reporting
#define MBEDTLS_ERROR_C

//used by lwIP
#define MBEDTLS_ENTROPY_C
#define MBEDTLS_CTR_DRBG_C

//RSA KEY EXCHANGE
#define MBEDTLS_KEY_EXCHANGE_RSA_ENABLED
#define MBEDTLS_RSA_C

//general key exchange
#define MBEDTLS_PKCS1_V15
#define MBEDTLS_BIGNUM_C
#define MBEDTLS_PK_C
#define MBEDTLS_PK_PARSE_C

//encryption
#define MBEDTLS_AES_C
#define MBEDTLS_CCM_C
#define MBEDTLS_CIPHER_MODE_CBC
#define MBEDTLS_AES_FEWER_TABLES

//certs
#define MBEDTLS_X509_CRT_PARSE_C
#define MBEDTLS_X509_USE_C
#define MBEDTLS_OID_C
#define MBEDTLS_ASN1_PARSE_C
#define MBEDTLS_ASN1_WRITE_C

//hash methods
#define MBEDTLS_SHA1_C
#define MBEDTLS_SHA224_C
#define MBEDTLS_SHA256_C
#define MBEDTLS_SHA512_C
```

```
//TLS
#define MBEDTLS_CIPHER_C
#define MBEDTLS_SSL_TLS_C
#define MBEDTLS_MD_C

//enable client and server modes and TLS
#define MBEDTLS_SSL_CLI_C
#define MBEDTLS_SSL_SERVER_NAME_INDICATION

//enable TLS 1.2
#define MBEDTLS_SSL_PROTO_TLS1_2

#include
"/home/pi/pico/pico-sdk/lib/mbedtls/include/mbedtls/check_config.h"
```

The configuration file has been divided into sections. The first is necessary because lwIP makes use of the features so they have to be included. The Key Exchange section specifies the RSA key exchange with a number of other defines that are dependencies. The encryption section enables AES with CBC and CCM, see the next chapter for information on what these are. The certificate handling and hash methods sections are standard. Next we turn on TLS, these defines have to be included to turn TLS on at all. We also define client mode and SNI, Server Name Indication, to send the server name to the server. Finally we enable TLS 1.2.

The very final line is worth knowing about this includes the check_config.h file which will run a check on the rest of the configuration. It will report any settings which don't have all of their dependent settings enabled and it will report any conflicts. It makes creating an mbedtls_config.h file much easier than just trying to find out what everything does by reading the comments in the config.h file in /pico/pico-sdk/lib/mbedtls/include/mbedtls/. Of course, you need to modify the path so that it can be found.

It is worth knowing that modifying the configuration file needs a clean rebuild.

The only other file we need to modify is the `CmakeLists.txt` file:

```
cmake_minimum_required(VERSION 3.13)
set(PICO_BOARD pico_w)
set(CMAKE_C_STANDARD 11)
set(CMAKE_CXX_STANDARD 17)

include(pico_sdk_import.cmake)
project(PicoW C CXX ASM)
pico_sdk_init()

add_executable(main
 main.c
)

target_include_directories(main PRIVATE ${CMAKE_CURRENT_LIST_DIR})

target_link_libraries(main pico_stdlib
pico_cyw43_arch_lwip_threadsafe_background pico_lwip_mbedtls
pico_mbedtls)
pico_add_extra_outputs(main)
```

All we really have to do is add `pico_lwip_mbedtls` and `pico_mbedtls` to the target libraries.

The Simple HTTPS Client Listing

Putting all this together we need to create a project with the following files:

`main.c`	full listing below
`lwipopts.h`	add the lines given earlier to the examples `lwipopts` file
`mbedtls_config.h`	full listing given earlier
`pico_sdk_import_cmake`	unmodified standard file in all Pico projects
`CmakeLists.txt`	full listing given earlier
`setupWiFi.h`	standard connection file given earlier

The full main.c is:

```c
#include <stdio.h>
#include "pico/stdlib.h"
#include "pico/cyw43_arch.h"

#include "lwip/altcp.h"
#include "lwip/altcp_tls.h"

#include "setupWifi.h"

#define BUF_SIZE 2048
char myBuff[BUF_SIZE];
char header[] = "GET /index.html HTTP/1.1\r\n
                              HOST:example.com\r\n\r\n";

err_t recv(void *arg, struct altcp_pcb *pcb,
                                 struct pbuf *p, err_t err)
{

    if (p != NULL)
    {
        printf("recv total %d  this buffer %d next %d err %d\n",
                              p->tot_len, p->len, p->next, err);
        pbuf_copy_partial(p, myBuff, p->tot_len, 0);
        myBuff[p->tot_len] = 0;
        printf("Buffer= %s\n", myBuff);
        altcp_recved(pcb, p->tot_len);
        pbuf_free(p);
    }
    return ERR_OK;
}

static err_t altcp_client_connected(void *arg,
                              struct altcp_pcb *pcb, err_t err)
{
    err = altcp_write(pcb, header, strlen(header), 0);
    err = altcp_output(pcb);
    return ERR_OK;
}
```

```
int main()
{
    stdio_init_all();
    connect();

    struct altcp_tls_config *tls_config =
                        altcp_tls_create_config_client(NULL, 0);
    struct altcp_pcb *pcb = altcp_tls_new(tls_config,
                                            IPADDR_TYPE_ANY);
    mbedtls_ssl_set_hostname(altcp_tls_context(pcb),
                                            "example.com");

    altcp_recv(pcb, recv);

    ip_addr_t ip;
    IP4_ADDR(&ip, 93, 184, 216, 34);
    cyw43_arch_lwip_begin();
    err_t err = altcp_connect(pcb, &ip, 443,
                                    altcp_client_connected);
    cyw43_arch_lwip_end();
    while (true)
    {
        sleep_ms(500);
    }
}
```

Non-blocking HTTPS Request

Now that we have a simple HTTPS client working, it is time to modify the non-blocking request function constructed in the previous chapter. As the only real difference is the way the PCB is constructed the changes are surprisingly small. We only have to modify the newConnection function, but in this case providing a separate newTLSConnection is a reasonable way of doing the job:

```
struct connectionState *newTLSConnection(char* host,
                    char *sendData, int bytes, char *recvData)
{
    struct connectionState *cs = (struct connectionState *)
                        malloc(sizeof(struct connectionState));
    cs->state = 0;

    struct altcp_tls_config *tls_config =
                        altcp_tls_create_config_client(NULL, 0);
    cs->pcb = altcp_tls_new(tls_config, IPADDR_TYPE_ANY);
    mbedtls_ssl_set_hostname(altcp_tls_context(cs->pcb), host);

    altcp_recv(cs->pcb, recv);
    altcp_sent(cs->pcb, sent);
    altcp_err(cs->pcb, err);
    altcp_poll(cs->pcb, poll, 10);
    altcp_arg(cs->pcb, cs);
```

```
    cs->sendData = sendData;
    cs->bytes=bytes;
    cs->recvData = recvData;
    cs->start = 0;
    return cs;
}
```

Only the three lines in the middle are new, but notice that we also need to pass in the host name to allow the TLS connection to ask for the correct certificate. It is also reasonable to provide a separate doTLSRequestBinary:

```
struct connectionState *doTLSRequestBinary(ip_addr_t *ip,
      char *host, u16_t port, char *request, char *file,
                         char *sendData,int bytes, char *recvData)
{
    char headerTemplate[] = "%s %s HTTP/1.1\r\n
                             HOST:%s:%d\r\n
                             Connection: close\r\n
                             Content-length: %d\r\n\r\n";
    int len = snprintf(NULL, 0, headerTemplate,
                            request, file, host, port, bytes);
    char *requestData = malloc(len + bytes+1);
    snprintf(requestData, len+1, headerTemplate,
                            request, file, host, port, bytes);
    memcpy(requestData+len,sendData,bytes);

    struct connectionState *cs =
        newTLSConnection(host,requestData,len+bytes ,recvData);
    cyw43_arch_lwip_begin();
    err_t err = altcp_connect(cs->pcb, ip, port, connected);
    cyw43_arch_lwip_end();
    cs->state = 1;
    return cs;
}
```

Using these two modifications to the request.h file, a main program to download example.com is:

```c
#include <stdio.h>

#include "pico/stdlib.h"
#include "pico/cyw43_arch.h"
#include "lwip/pbuf.h"
#include "lwip/altcp_tcp.h"
#include "lwip/altcp_tls.h"
#include "setupWifi.h"

#include "request.h"

#define BUF_SIZE 2048
char myBuff[BUF_SIZE];

int main()
{

    stdio_init_all();
    connect();

    ip_addr_t ip;
    IP4_ADDR(&ip, 93, 184, 216, 34);

    struct connectionState *cs1 = doTLSRequestBinary(&ip,
                "example.com", 443, "GET", "/", NULL, 0, myBuff);
    while (pollRequest(&cs1))
    {
        sleep_ms(200);
    }
    printf("%s\n", myBuff);

    return 0;
}
```

Notice that we are using a binary request, but for a GET we pass a NULL send buffer and set the length to 0.

None of the configuration files need to be changed.

The full program listing can be found on this book's page at www.iopress.info.

It would be quite easy to implement a HTTPS temperature sensor client or a binary client using this version of request.h, but implementing a custom HTTPS server in Python needs knowledge of creating a certificate so this is postponed until Chapter 6.

Summary

- Public key cryptography works with two keys, a private key and a public key, and hence is called asymmetric key cryptography. The public key is not secret and can be used by anyone to encrypt a text. The encrypted text can only be decrypted using the private key which is kept secret.

- Symmetric key cryptography uses a single key which has to be kept private to the sender and receiver to encrypt and decrypt text.

- Symmetric key cryptography is much faster than asymmetric and so what happens is that asymmetric keys are used to establish a single secret symmetric key that both the client and server use.

- A certificate contains identity information and keys.

- A client and a server can establish encrypted communication in one of two ways. If both have a certificate then the keys are used to exchange a single symmetric key. If only the server has a certificate then this is used by both parties to construct a shared secret key.

- SSL, which later evolved into TSL, is used to add encryption to sockets. The lwIP RAW doesn't use sockets but it can still make use of TLS to implement HTTPS via ALTCP.

- To implement TLS you need to use ALTCP and the mbedtls library. The connection between the two is the altcp_tls library.

- To configure mbedtls you need to use the `mbedtls_config.h` file to define the encryption methods you want to use.

- The most commonly encountered methods are RSA key exchange followed by AES symmetric encryption.

- Putting all this together it is easy to create an HTTPS client without the need to work with certificates.

Chapter 5

Details of Cryptography

Cryptography is hard and you need to be an expert to implement almost any of its methods, however you also need to be a little bit of an expert to understand what the choices are in making use of a library like mbedtls. This chapter is a collection of theory and practice concerning the various things you have to get right to ensure that you are using the cryptography provided by the library in a secure way. This is by no means a complete or advanced treatment and at the end of the chapter there is still much to know but you should be able to appreciate some of the difficulties in achieving and maintaining security. It's a "get you started" practical guide.

The Problem of Random Numbers

One of the requirements of IoT devices that are intended for anything other than personal or experimental use is ensuring that the device is secure. The best way to do this is to use a well-known and widely used cryptographic library such as mbedtls. If you do this you can claim "uses industry standard" encryption. Unfortunately all of the security rests on the foundation of a good random number source.

The reason for this is not difficult to see. The random numbers are used to generate the key used in the symmetric key encryption used to transmit the bulk of the data between client and server. The public and private key encryption which doesn't rely on a random number generation is secure as long as you keep the private key secret and as long as it has enough bits to make working it out from the public key or guessing it difficult.

Symmetric key encryption, on the other hand, is vulnerable to simply guessing the key. You can try to decrypt the data using trial keys until you get something intelligible as plain text. Again this is difficult as long as the key has enough bits and has been chosen at random. However, if the random number generator has any statistical flaws then the search space of trial keys can be much reduced. For example, any random number generator that delivers more zeros than ones cuts the search space in half. If you can find enough statistical irregularities you can reduce the initial huge search space into something more reasonable.

In short, the security of symmetric key encryption depends on the quality of the random number generator.

The question is how much quality do you need in a random number generator?

In practice, the chance of a device being hacked due to a not-quite-perfect random number generator is small because it generally isn't worth the effort and there are lots of easier ways to compromise a system, especially if you have physical access to it. However, there is also the matter of how things are presented. Some users are very security-conscious and the only reasonable way of satisfying them is to use industry standard encryption with industry standard best practices. If you have to state "we use a standard cryptographic library but use a homemade random number generator" then confidence will be dented.

To make use of TLS you have to provide a random number generator, `mbedtls_hardware_poll`, to enable the key exchange to work. With the introduction of SDK 1.5 there are a number of new random number generating functions and a standard implementation of `mbedtls_hardware_poll` is made available using them. However, this doesn't mean you can ignore the problem. Random numbers are important and understanding the problem is worth the investment.

Pseudo Randomness

The first distinction to be made is the difference between a pseudo random number generator (PRNG) and a true random number generator. A pseudo random number generator is just an algorithm that produces numbers that "look" random. Each number occurs with equal frequency and there is no connection between one number generated and another that would help you predict one from the other. For example, while a simple for loop generates numbers that are equally probable 0,1,2,3,4,5,6,7,8,9 and so on, it is a very poor pseudo random number generator because as soon as I tell you the current value is 5 you can work out the that the next number is 6.

Clearly the difficulty here is in defining what we method we can use to predict the values. If you know the algorithm in use you can always predict the next or any value that will be produced. In this sense no pseudo random number generator is truly random. Even though this is obviously the case, pseudo random number generators are useful.

The sequence that a PRNG produces depends on where it is started from. The starting value is usually called the "seed" and starting from a fixed seed always produces the same sequence. There are situations where this is useful and some where it is definitely to be avoided. For example, if you are programming a card game using a PRNG and use the same seed to start it off each time the program is run, the players will be subjected to the same sequence of cards. In this case, you need some mechanism to select a different seed each time the program is run. On the other hand, if you are testing a set of alternatives to see how they perform then using the same sequence of pseudo random numbers for each test is much more informative than using truly random numbers.

Even though pseudo random numbers are generated by an algorithm, we can still perform statistical tests on them and look for statistical relationships that can help with guessing the next number. For example, if the PRNG tends to produce an odd number after an even number then we can use this to improve our guessing of the next number. However, if you know the type of PRNG being used then you might be able to use a small sample of random numbers to work out exactly what is being used and hence predict all of the subsequent numbers exactly. This defect is not shared by hardware random number generators.

There are many approaches to creating a PRNG, but two are particularly important for small machines and form the basis for most complicated algorithms – the Linear Congruential Generator (LCG) and the Linear-feedback Shift Register (LFSR). In both cases, given samples of random numbers from the generator you can work out its exact setup and generate subsequent numbers accurately.

The standard C function rand is an LCG PRNG. The call:

```
r = rand();
```

returns the next integer in the sequence. If you want to set a seed then you use:

```
srand(seed);
```

If you don't specify a seed then 1 is used and rand produces a sequence that is so well known it is listed and recognized by The On-Line Encyclopedia of Integer Sequences. It may have random properties, but it is still well known and anyone recognizing it can easily give you any values in the sequence in any order. In fact, the version of rand supplied with GCC is good enough to pass the standard tests of randomness, see later, but it is still unusable as a random number generator to use with mbedtls as its generator is too easy to identify.

Hardware Random Generator

The obvious thing to do to obtain a cryptographic random number generator is to use hardware to produce real physical random numbers. Truly random numbers are not predictable no matter how many samples you take even if you know how they are generated. In this sense a perfect hardware random number generator (HRNG) is what we need. Of course, any physicist will tell you that the only source of truly random numbers is quantum mechanics. Some electronic devices can generate randomness based on quantum effects, but in practice you generally don't need to be so esoteric. We regularly treat complex physical systems as if they were truly random. When you toss a coin you regard the outcome as random, but in principle if you could measure the initial position of the coin, the force used to propel it into the air and the disposition of the ground, you could work out which side it would land on. In practice, of course, you can't and there are physical systems that are so sensitive to the initial conditions that, even if you knew them accurately, accurate prediction would be difficult. In this sense even physical sources or randomness only produce pseudo random numbers – if you knew the generating algorithm you could predict them. In practice of course you don't and you can't and so hardware generated random numbers are what we need.

In practice, physical sources of noise or entropy can be very simple. For example, you can take readings from an analog to digital converter that isn't connected to anything or measure the voltage on a reverse-biased diode etc. The problem with all of these ideas is that they are easily spoiled by interactions with the outside world. For example reading data from an unconnected AtoD is vulnerable to whatever coherent signal the input picks up as it acts as an aerial. Similarly timers, often used as sources of random bits, no matter how erratic they tend to be, show short range correlations in output.

In short, actually designing a good physical source of entropy that provides good random numbers is much more difficult than theory suggests. A hardware source of random numbers that has statistical regularities can be predicted in the same way that imperfect pseudo random numbers can.

Cryptographic Random Generator

Now that we have considered the two major types of random number generators and their strengths and failings we can consider what would make a good generator. A cryptographic random number generator (CRNG) is usually defined as one where it has been proved that any algorithm that can predict the $n+1$ value with a better than 50% chance of being right given n values has to take more than polynomial time. The idea is that even if there is a prediction method it will be so slow as to be impractical.

A second condition requires that even if part of its internal state has been revealed or guessed then it should be impossible to reconstruct the sequence. This means that a congruential generator is ruled out on both counts, as is an LFSR. Just appearing to be random isn't enough to be a CRNG. You have to have a cast iron guarantee that no matter how many samples are gathered you cannot deduce the algorithm used to generate them in anything like a reasonable time.

A CRNG not only has to pass the first test of appearing to be random, it also has to not reveal details of how the values are generated. It might seem that any algorithmic method of generating random number cannot be a CRNG as there is an algorithm to be discovered. There are provably secure CRNGs based on mathematical problems known to be hard to solve. For example, the Blum Blum Shub algorithm produces a sequence based on the quadratic residue problem which is not solvable in polynomial time. In this case having a sample from the sequence is provably difficult to reverse engineer in the sense that it would take an attacker too long to go from values in the sequence to the parameters of the mechanism that created it.

In short, algorithmic CRNGs do exist. However, while it is good to know that such things exist they are mostly not practical for IoT use due to their computational demands.

An additional consideration, not normally discussed in the literature, is that in many cases an IoT device is in the hands of the end user. That is, IoT devices are generally not physically secure. What this means is that if you program a cryptographically sound random number generator then it is only a matter of time before someone reverse engineers your device and the details of the generator are accurately known including the configuration parameters. This means that any PRNG, CRNG or not, is insecure when installed in an IoT device.

The only practical approach is to make use of an algorithm to improve the statistical qualities of an HRNG. In this case you can make the argument that the good statistical qualities makes it hard for an attacker to guess the next number and even if they had a set of numbers from the sequence the hardware generated component makes this knowledge useless in predicting future values.

What all this means is that, contrary to what you will often read, for an IoT device the task is not to install a CRNG that is provably secure, but to improve any HRNG sufficiently to make it pass a battery of statistical tests of randomness.

There are three general approaches to enhancing a hardware source of randomness:

1. You can use a randomness extractor – an algorithm that makes the HRNG even more random. For example, you could XOR the output of the HRNG with the output of a good PRNG. Even if you know the details of the PRNG you still can't reliably predict subsequent numbers.

2. Hash functions and encryption methods are designed to break up patterns in the source text and these can be applied to the output of a HRNG to improve its statistical properties. This is the reason you will often encounter the strange idea of encrypting or hashing hardware generated random numbers. You can use multiple HRNGs and combine them together to produce numbers with better statistical properties. This is often called using an entropy pool and it is an approach that has become very popular – Linux uses it, for example, to implement dev/random and dev/urandom.

Testing Random Numbers

Before you decide to use any random number generator you need to either test it yourself or rely on tests already performed to confirm that it is indeed generating random numbers. The only problem with this is that there are a number of libraries of testing software and they are are poorly supported. The best known are diehard, dieharder and the NIST. None of them are particularly easy to use, but at least if your random numbers pass enough of the NIST suite you can claim that you are using something that passes the National Institute of Standards and Technology.

To test random numbers you need to generate a large sample – 100,000 or more and consider the potential weaknesses of the generator according to the tests that they fail.

Harnessing Entropy

The Pico has a source of entropy in the form of a Ring Oscillator (ROSC). It is basically a clock that runs at a rate that varies according to temperature and operating voltage etc. This means that reading it can provide a moderately random value. The data sheet says:

> "If the system clocks are running from the XOSC and/or PLLs the ROSC can be used to generate random numbers. Simply enable the ROSC and read the RANDOMBIT register to get a 1-bit random number and read it n times to get an nbit value. This does not meet the requirements of randomness for security systems because it can be compromised, but it may be useful in less critical applications. If the cores are running from the ROSC then the value will not be random because the timing of the register read will be correlated to the phase of the ROSC. "

In a standard Pico the clock is derived from the XOSC and the ROSC can be used to supply a random bit. This is very easy to do. To access the correct register all you need is:

```
#include "hardware/structs/rosc.h"
```

which imports a struct that has the correct address assigned to a pointer. After this you can read a random bit using:

```
bit = rosc_hw->randombit
```

The bit is returned as the low order bit of a 32-bit int.

You can create a random byte using:

```
uint8_t randomByte()
{
    uint32_t random = 0;
    for (int k = 0; k < 8; k++)
    {
      random = (random << 1) | rosc_hw->randombit;
    }
    return (uint8_t)random;
}
```

If you try this out you will find that it fails most of the NIST tests of randomness. It doesn't even pass the test for an equal number of ones and zeros. The probability of generating a zero is 0.55 which is a small, but significant, bias.

A simple transformation, called von Neumann whitening after its inventor, improves the balance of ones and zeros. If you have a bit stream with unequal probabilities of a one or a zero you can transform it to a 0 on a change from 0 to 1 and a 1 on a change from 1 to 0 and discard bits pairs of bits that are equal, i.e. 00 and 11. There are obviously as many up-going edges as there are down-going edges so the number of ones and zeros is the same. The cost of this transformation is needing a few more random bits to throw away:

```
uint8_t randomByte()
{
    uint32_t random = 0;
    uint32_t bit = 0;
    for (int k = 0; k < 8; k++)
    {
                while (true)
                {
                    bit = rosc_hw->randombit;
                    if (bit != rosc_hw->randombit)
                        break;
                }

                random = (random << 1) | bit;
    return (uint8_t)random;
}
```

If you try this out you will discover that it only reduces the bias to 0.54 and the random sequence still fails the NIST tests. The reason is that the sequential bits are correlated.

The problem is that the ROSC is a source of entropy but we are taking data from it too fast. The oscillator varies over time and to reduce the correlations between subsequent bits we need to allow enough time between readings for the oscillator to have randomly drifted. Putting this another way the entropy accumulates with time.

The solution is to modify the von Neumann whitening to include a delay:

```
uint8_t randomByte()
{
    uint32_t random = 0;
    uint32_t bit = 0;
    for (int k = 0; k < 8; k++)
    {
                while (true)
                {
                    bit = rosc_hw->randombit;
                    sleep_us(10);
                    if (bit != rosc_hw->randombit)
                        break;
                }
                random = (random << 1) | bit;
                sleep_us(10);
    }
    return (uint8_t)random;
}
```

This produces a random sequence that passes all of the NIST tests and has virtually no bias – the probability of a zero bit is 0.499. The delay could possibly be reduced, but if you only want a few tens of random bytes this isn't worth optimizing. With this delay the ROSC becomes an acceptable source of randomness that you can use to generate keys.

Pico SDK Randomness

The mbedtls library has a facility to combine multiple sources of entropy, but the Pico SDK has opted not to implement this. Instead the SDK 1.5 includes a new set of random functions which combine a range of different sources of entropy. There are three new functions:

- `uint64_t get_rand_64(void)`
- `uint32_t get_rand_32(void)`
- `void get_rand_128(rng_128_t *ptr128)`

which return random numbers with the specified number of bits. The 64-bit numbers are used to generate 32- and 128-bit numbers by throwing away the top 32 bits and calling the function twice respectively. For an example of using `get_rand_128` see the AES ECB program later in this chapter.

The 64-bit generator uses an entropy pooling approach with three sources:

◆ the ring oscillator (ROSC)

◆ the 64-bit microsecond timer

◆ the bus performance counter

You can disable them, and even configure how they are used, via a number of defines, but apart from turning the ROSC off if it is being used by the processor you are well advised to leave them at their default values.

Each of the sources is hashed before being used to improve its statistical properties and is then applied to the output of a high quality PRNG.

The PRNG is seeded using random bits gathered when the random number functions are first used – this is slow and can take up to 1ms to seed the PRNG. After this random number generation takes between 10 and $20\mu s$. The entropy sources used for seeding are different from generating random numbers:

◆ the Ring Oscillator (ROSC)

◆ the 64-bit microsecond timer

◆ the Board Identifier

◆ the RAM hash

You can configure the entropy sources used for seeding separately from those used for subsequent random number generation.

The `pico_rand` library can be used standalone, but note that if you really need pseudo random numbers this isn't what you want – use the standard rand function instead with a suitable seed.

The pico_rand library passes all of the NIST tests but only if you are using SDK 1.51 or you manually patch an error in SDK 1.50.

SDK 1.50 contains an error which causes the random numbers to be biased towards zero. To correct this edit:

pico/pico-sdk/src/rp2_common/pico_rand/rand.c

to change line 275:

```
local_rng_state.r[which] &= splitmix64(bus_counter_value);
```

to read:

```
local_rng_state.r[which] ^= splitmix64(bus_counter_value);
```

That is, change & to ^. Do not use `pico_rand` without this correction.

What is interesting is that `pico_rand` doesn't perform significantly differently to the simple ROSC-based generator given earlier, but its complexity and sophistication probably inspire more confidence.

The random number function that mbedtls uses, as defined in `pico/pico-sdk/src/rp2_common/pico_mbedtls/pico_mbedtls.c`, is:

```
#include <string.h>
#include "pico/platform.h"
#include "pico/rand.h"

/* Function to feed mbedtls entropy. */
int mbedtls_hardware_poll(void *data __unused,
          unsigned char *output, size_t len, size_t *olen) {
 *olen = 0;
 while(*olen < len) {
    uint64_t rand_data = get_rand_64();
    size_t to_copy = MIN(len, sizeof(rand_data));
    memcpy(output + *olen, &rand_data, to_copy);
    *olen += to_copy;
 }
 return 0;
}
```

Random numbers are the foundation of good security, but what you do with them also matters.

What Encryption Suite?

If you experiment with the HTTPS client program, you will find that it works on example.com and on many other websites, but it is possible that you will find a website that is using TLS 1.3, or a more advanced key exchange or encryption method, that you do not support.

Most servers support as wide a range of encryption standards as possible, but encryption methods that are considered insecure are usually left out of the mix. Some servers restrict the encryption methods a client can use to only the most secure in an attempt to improve their overall security. For example, you will find websites that only support the latest version of TLS and, as mbedtls doesn't support TLS 1.3, there isn't much you can do about connecting to such servers if they select a method that isn't supported in TLS 1.2 or simply reject the connection.

The usual solution for implementing a client is to include as many cryptographic methods as possible hoping that they support one of the methods that the server can work with, no matter how rarely encountered. If you are programming an IoT device then this approach is possible, but wasteful. Each crypto method you support increases the size and complexity of your program. In most cases it is better to restrict the methods to just those used by the servers you are trying to connect to. In particular, if the server is one that is under your control then you can select a single encryption method that works on both the client and the server.

An encryption suite is a combined set of cryptographic methods.

The big problem is that there are are lots of alternative methods and they are identified using acronyms that are cryptic if you don't know what they mean. Here is a brief and incomplete guide:

RSA	Rivest Shamir Adleman public key encryption
CAMELLIA	public key cipher alternative to RSA
AES	Advanced Encryption Standard
ECB	Electronic codebook block cipher mode
CBC	Cipher Block Chaining block cipher mode
CCM	Counter with Cipher block chaining Message authentication
GCM	Galois Counter Mode for message authentication
DH or DHE	Diffie Hellman key exchange
ECDH or ECDHE	Elliptic curve Diffie Hellman key exchange
PSK	Preshared Key used as a prefix/suffix as in PSK-RSA
SRP	Secure Remote Password
DSA	Digital Signature Algorithm
SHA n	a set of hash functions

A particular suite is generally written as a list in the order:

Key exchange-Authentication-Encryption method-Hash

So, for example, the TLS suite:

TLS_ECDHE_ECDSA_WITH_AES_128_GCM_SHA256

uses elliptic curve Diffie Hellman key exchange, elliptic curve authentication, AES with a 128-bit key and GCM mode and SHA256 for a hash.

All of this raises the question of how to find out what encryption method or encryption suite a particular server supports. The only way to do this is to write a program that attempts to connect to the server using each possible suite in turn. You could do this using mbedtls but it is much easier to use an off-the-shelf script or application. There are many to choose between but nmap is generally useful, easy to install and has a testing script included.

You can install nmap on Windows from `https://nmap.org/`.

Installation on the Raspberry Pi is also easy:

```
sudo apt update
sudo apt install nmap
```

Once you have nmap installed you can check that encryption suites offered by any website using:

```
nmap -sV --script ssl-enum-ciphers -p 443 host
```

where *host* is an IP address or a URL.

If you run the command on example.com you will see something like:

```
PORT   STATE SERVICE  VERSION
443/tcp open  ssl/http Edgecast CDN httpd (dcb/7F14)
| http-server-header:
|   ECS (dcb/7F37)
|_  ECS (dcb/7F82)
| ssl-enum-ciphers:
```
reports for TLSv1.0 and TLSv1.1 removed
```
|   TLSv1.2:
|     ciphers:
|       TLS_ECDHE_RSA_WITH_AES_128_GCM_SHA256 (secp256r1) - A
|       TLS_ECDHE_RSA_WITH_AES_256_GCM_SHA384 (secp256r1) - A
|       TLS_DHE_RSA_WITH_AES_128_GCM_SHA256 (dh 2048) - A
|       TLS_DHE_RSA_WITH_AES_256_GCM_SHA384 (dh 2048) - A
|       TLS_ECDHE_RSA_WITH_AES_128_CBC_SHA256 (secp256r1) - A
|       TLS_ECDHE_RSA_WITH_AES_128_CBC_SHA (secp256r1) - A
|       TLS_ECDHE_RSA_WITH_AES_256_CBC_SHA384 (secp256r1) - A
|       TLS_ECDHE_RSA_WITH_AES_256_CBC_SHA (secp256r1) - A
|       TLS_DHE_RSA_WITH_AES_128_CBC_SHA256 (dh 2048) - A
|       TLS_DHE_RSA_WITH_AES_128_CBC_SHA (dh 2048) - A
|       TLS_DHE_RSA_WITH_AES_256_CBC_SHA256 (dh 2048) - A
|       TLS_DHE_RSA_WITH_AES_256_CBC_SHA (dh 2048) - A
|       TLS_RSA_WITH_AES_128_GCM_SHA256 (rsa 2048) - A
|       TLS_DHE_RSA_WITH_CAMELLIA_256_CBC_SHA (dh 2048) - A
|       TLS_DHE_RSA_WITH_CAMELLIA_128_CBC_SHA (dh 2048) - A
|       TLS_RSA_WITH_AES_256_CBC_SHA (rsa 2048) - A
|       TLS_RSA_WITH_CAMELLIA_256_CBC_SHA (rsa 2048) - A
|       TLS_RSA_WITH_AES_128_CBC_SHA (rsa 2048) - A
|       TLS_RSA_WITH_CAMELLIA_128_CBC_SHA (rsa 2048) - A
|       TLS_DHE_RSA_WITH_SEED_CBC_SHA (dh 2048) - A
|       TLS_RSA_WITH_SEED_CBC_SHA (rsa 2048) - A
|     compressors:
|       NULL
|     cipher preference: server
|_  least strength: A

Service detection performed. Please report any incorrect results at https://nmap.org/submit/ .
Nmap done: 1 IP address (1 host up) scanned in 31.70 seconds
```

You can see that it lists all of the methods and gives them a strength rating, reporting the least strong. In this case all of the supported methods rate an A and we might as well use any of them. The one we have opted to support in the client is TLS_RSA_WITH_AES_256_CBC_SHA (rsa 2048).

If you connect to a server that uses this suite, Chrome complains in the Security tab of the Inspector:

Connection – obsolete connection settings.

RSA key exchange is obsolete. Enable ECDHE based cipher suite.

AES_256_CBC is obsolete. Enable an AES-GCM based cipher suite.

If you want to take this advice, see the next section. Notice that the Security tab in Chrome can also be used to find out what suite is being used for a connection.

Adding Encryption Suites

In most cases there are enough resources to support a good range of encryption suites. If you want to add more then you have to add them to mbedtls_config.h. The best way to discover what suites and methods are supported is to read the

pico/pico-sdk/lib/mbedtls/include/mbedtls/config.h

file which is so well documented with comments that the problem is finding your way through it.

There is also a Python command line utility, config.py, that can be used to change settings or create standard configurations. You can find this in pico/pico-sdk/lib/mbedtls/scripts. In most cases the standard configurations don't suit the Pico and it is easier to directly edit the configuration file.

If you want to add support for a particular cryptographic function then the simplest way is to find the main configuration parameter for it. For example, elliptic curve cryptography is said to be fast and efficient. Indeed Chrome will complain that you are not using the latest cipher suite when running a server without it, see the next chapter. To keep Chrome happy we need to support an ECDHE and AES-GCM-based cipher suite.

If you want to enable ECDHE for key exchange then a quick search on ECDHE in the config.h file finds:

#define MBEDTLS_KEY_EXCHANGE_ECDHE_RSA_ENABLED

which enables both elliptic curve Diffie Hellman key exchange and digital signature. The RSA part is needed for certificate validation – we are using an RSA certificate. There are many other ECDHE-supporting suites but this is the one we need and in many cases there is no choice but to read through all the possibilities and weed out the ones that do not include everything we require.

Adding this to the configuration file isn't the end of the story, however, as it has dependencies. This will be pointed out to you if try to build the program with:

```
#include
"/home/pi/pico/pico-sdk/lib/mbedtls/include/mbedtls/check_config.h"
```

and you will be told what the dependencies are. In this case we also have to add to what we already have in the configuration file:

```
#define MBEDTLS_ECDH_C
#define MBEDTLS_ECDSA_C
```

This too is insufficient as `MBEDTLS_ECDSA_C` has dependencies which are missing from our configuration file, namely:

```
#define MBEDTLS_ECP_C
```

and any one or more of the many elliptic curves used for the code:

```
/* Short Weierstrass curves (supporting ECP, ECDH, ECDSA) */
#define MBEDTLS_ECP_DP_SECP192R1_ENABLED
#define MBEDTLS_ECP_DP_SECP224R1_ENABLED
#define MBEDTLS_ECP_DP_SECP256R1_ENABLED
#define MBEDTLS_ECP_DP_SECP384R1_ENABLED
#define MBEDTLS_ECP_DP_SECP521R1_ENABLED
#define MBEDTLS_ECP_DP_SECP192K1_ENABLED
#define MBEDTLS_ECP_DP_SECP224K1_ENABLED
#define MBEDTLS_ECP_DP_SECP256K1_ENABLED
#define MBEDTLS_ECP_DP_BP256R1_ENABLED
#define MBEDTLS_ECP_DP_BP384R1_ENABLED
#define MBEDTLS_ECP_DP_BP512R1_ENABLED
```

The question is which elliptic curves to support? Recall that the server and the client negotiate for a method that they both support, so this often isn't as critical a choice as it might appear. The most commonly supported are `SECP256K1` and `SECP384R1`. Other TLS libraries support all of the above curves.

Finally, to enable GCM mode we need to add:

```
#define MBEDTLS_GCM_C
```

If you make all of these additions, the complete configuration file is available on the book's web page, you will discover that Chrome stops complaining that we are using obsolete suites:

▥ Connection - secure connection settings

The connection to this site is encrypted and authenticated using TLS 1.2, ECDHE_RSA with P-384, and AES_256_GCM.

The P-384 indicates that the connection is using the SECP384R1 elliptic curve.

Including elliptic curve encryption increases the connection time to around five seconds and slows things down a lot. In most cases RSA key exchange is quite sufficient.

Symmetric Encryption

Now that the Pico has mbedtls it can be used for all sorts of cryptographic tasks independently of lwIP or any other library. For example, you can use it to encrypt and decrypt data without needing to use TLS. The most useful thing to do in this case is to use a symmetric encryption algorithm and assume that the problem of key exchange has been solved in some way or other. For an IoT device, using symmetric encryption has the advantage that you are only using a cheap-to-produce random key and not a public private key pair. In this way each device can have its own encryption key rather than a single key used by all devices. Of course, we still have the standard problem that if the IoT device is physically in the hands of an attacker then any key is easy enough to discover. If you're using a system where each device generates a fixed random key, at least its discovery would not compromise other devices. More importantly using your own symmetric encryption allows you to send the data over any type of connection, not just HTTPS, and store it safely on unsecured devices. As long as the key is kept private then so is the data. Of course, the flip side of this is that if you lose the key you have also lost the data.

In this example the encryption method used is AES, which is still considered to be a strong and effectively uncrackable as long as you use a large key size. At the time of writing, 128-bit and 256-bit keys are considered secure when used in conjunction with best practices. The keys cannot be broken from a sample of the encrypted text, but you can weaken them by accidentally providing information about them.

AES encryption is a block cipher which means that it encrypts a fixed size buffer of plain text. Any plain text has to be broken into blocks of the correct size and any that are too small have to be padded to make a complete block. There are a number of standard ways of padding a block but usually mbedtls will do the job for you.

There are a number of small variations or modes of AES that modify how blocks are processed. The simplest is ECB or Electronic Codebook Block. This is simple, but is is no longer used as it is insecure in a very obvious way. It simply makes use of the key to encrypt each block in turn. The problem with this is that if you encrypt two identical blocks then the cipher text will also be identical and this can be noticed by an attacker and used to infer information. Even so, it is worth implementing AES using ECB as an example because it is so simple.

AES ECB Encryption Decryption

Using any of the encryption methods supported by mbedtls follows similar lines.

Encryption is controlled by a cipher_context struct which needs to be initialized:

```
mbedtls_cipher_context_t cipher_ctx;
mbedtls_cipher_init(&cipher_ctx);
```

Each supported encryption method has a cipher_info struct that defines its operation. To use a particular method you have to first retrieve its cipher_info struct and use this to set the cipher_context struct:

```
const mbedtls_cipher_info_t *cipher_info;
cipher_info = mbedtls_cipher_info_from_string("AES-128-ECB");
ret = mbedtls_cipher_setup(&cipher_ctx, cipher_info);
```

You can see that for this example we have selected AES-128-ECB. This means that we need to create a 16-byte 128-bit key and we can use the pico_rand get_rand_128 function introduced earlier:

```
unsigned char key[16];
get_rand_128((rng_128_t*)key);
```

To use the key we have to store it in the cipher_context struct:

```
ret = mbedtls_cipher_setkey(&cipher_ctx, key, cipher_info-
>key_bitlen, MBEDTLS_ENCRYPT);
```

We could have specified the key length as 128, but retrieving it from the cipher_info struct makes this more general. Also notice that we set the encryption direction at this point – i.e. plain text to cipher text.

Notice that key size is set in bits, but block size is set in bytes.

Now we are all set to start encoding some data, but as this is a block cipher we have to initialize the `cipher_context` struct to be ready to process the first block:

```
ret = mbedtls_cipher_reset(&cipher_ctx);
```

You can start encrypting blocks of bytes, but you have to supply 16-byte blocks. The function to use is:

```
ret = mbedtls_cipher_update(&cipher_ctx, buffer,
                                        ilen, output, &olen);
```

where `buffer` has the plain text block and is `ilen` long and `output` is the computed cipher text and is `olen` long. For AES ECB `ilen` and `olen` are `16`, but this isn't generally true. If you pass a block smaller than the block size then the function returns an error. It is perfectly OK to pad the block with zeros, which is what happens if you use a C string in fixed size char array.

As an example we can encode a single 16-byte block:

```
char buffer[16] = "Hello World";
char output[16];
int olen;
ret = mbedtls_cipher_update(&cipher_ctx, buffer, 16,
                                        output, &olen);
```

We can decrypt the cipher text just as easily:

```
char plaintext[16];
ret = mbedtls_cipher_setkey(&cipher_ctx, key,
                    cipher_info->key_bitlen, MBEDTLS_DECRYPT);
ret = mbedtls_cipher_reset(&cipher_ctx);
mbedtls_cipher_update(&cipher_ctx, output, 16, plaintext, &olen);
```

You can see that this follows the same steps and the only difference is that it is set to `MBEDTLS_DECRYPT`.

Putting all this together with some instructions to display the cipher text and the reconstructed plain text gives:

```c
#include <stdio.h>
#include "pico/stdlib.h"
#include "mbedtls/cipher.h"

#include "pico/rand.h"

int main()
{
    stdio_init_all();
    int ret;

    mbedtls_cipher_context_t cipher_ctx;
    mbedtls_cipher_init(&cipher_ctx);

    const mbedtls_cipher_info_t *cipher_info;
    cipher_info = mbedtls_cipher_info_from_string("AES-128-ECB");
    ret = mbedtls_cipher_setup(&cipher_ctx, cipher_info);

    unsigned char key[16];
    get_rand_128((rng_128_t*)key );

    ret = mbedtls_cipher_setkey(&cipher_ctx, key,
                        cipher_info->key_bitlen, MBEDTLS_ENCRYPT);
    ret = mbedtls_cipher_reset(&cipher_ctx);

    char buffer[16] = "Hello World";
    char output[16];
    int olen;
    ret = mbedtls_cipher_update(&cipher_ctx, buffer, 16,
                                                output, &olen);

    printf("cipher text ");
    for (int i = 0; i < olen; i++)
    {
        printf("%02X", output[i]);
    }
    printf("\n");

    char plaintext[16];
    ret = mbedtls_cipher_setkey(&cipher_ctx, key,
                        cipher_info->key_bitlen, MBEDTLS_DECRYPT);
    ret = mbedtls_cipher_reset(&cipher_ctx);
    mbedtls_cipher_update(&cipher_ctx, output, 16,
                                                plaintext, &olen);
    printf("plain text %.16s\n", plaintext);
    return 0;
}
```

Notice that the header files have been reduced to just what is required to run the program and, in the same spirit, the Cmakelists.txt file can be reduced to:

```
cmake_minimum_required(VERSION 3.13)
set(PICO_BOARD pico_w)
set(CMAKE_C_STANDARD 11)
set(CMAKE_CXX_STANDARD 17)

include(pico_sdk_import.cmake)
project(PicoW C CXX ASM)
pico_sdk_init()

add_executable(main
 main.c
)
target_include_directories(main PRIVATE ${CMAKE_CURRENT_LIST_DIR})

target_link_libraries(main pico_stdlib pico_mbedtls)
pico_add_extra_outputs(main)
```

Notice that we haven't bothered building lwIP mbedtls as it isn't being used. The original Cmakelists.txt will work, but it builds more code than we use.

We can also reduce the mbedtls configuration file to just the components we are using:

```
//Hardware config
#define MBEDTLS_NO_PLATFORM_ENTROPY
#define MBEDTLS_ENTROPY_HARDWARE_ALT
#define MBEDTLS_HAVE_TIME
//error reporting
#define MBEDTLS_ERROR_C
//encryption
#define MBEDTLS_AES_C
#define MBEDTLS_CCM_C
#define MBEDTLS_CIPHER_MODE_CBC
#define MBEDTLS_AES_FEWER_TABLES
#define MBEDTLS_CIPHER_C
#include
"/home/pi/pico/pico-sdk/lib/mbedtls/include/mbedtls/check_config.h"
```

Again you can use the previous mbedtls_config.h file – it will work, but enables features we don't need. If you try it out you will see the plain text and cipher text displayed. You can extend the program to process multiple blocks, but notice that they all have to be 16 bytes. To send or save the encrypted data, all you have to do is concatenate them into a larger block. As long as the decryption client can split them into blocks and has the key, everything works. Also notice that in this mode you can encrypt and decrypt blocks in any order as they are independent of one another.

AES CBC Mode

The previous program generates cipher text that is difficult to decrypt unless you have the key, but it doesn't do a good job of hiding the information. The problem is that if you encrypt two identical blocks you generate identical cipher text. In some situations this isn't a big security problem. In others it can invalidate the attempt at encryption. The best known example is using the ECB mode to encrypt an image:

Despite this image being encrypted using AES ECB you can see that it is the Linux mascot, Tux. The problem is that for an image the encryption has only managed to change the color of each of the encrypted blocks.

There are a number of block encryption modes that solve the problem by adding known but variable data to each block before it is encrypted. The simplest is CBC, Cipher Block Chaining. This XORs the previous cipher text with the plain text before encrypting it. This means that even if you encrypt the same plain text you get a different result. Decryption is still possible as you simply decrypt the block and then XOR it with the plain text of the previous block to recover the plain text. The only problem is what do you do about getting the process started, i.e. what do you XOR with the first block? The answer is that you have to provide an Initialization Vector (IV) which acts as a block zero and is XORed with the plain text of the first block. This also has to be made available to anyone wanting to decrypt a set of blocks. The IV is usually added to the list of blocks as a block zero.

Changing our previous program to use CBC is fairly simple. First we need to select an CBC encryption:

```
mbedtls_cipher_context_t cipher_ctx;
mbedtls_cipher_init(&cipher_ctx);
cipher_info = mbedtls_cipher_info_from_string("AES-128-CBC");
ret = mbedtls_cipher_setup(&cipher_ctx, cipher_info);
```

We have to create an IV and this can be just 16 bytes of random data:

```
unsigned char IV[16];
get_rand_128((rng_128_t*)IV );
ret = mbedtls_cipher_set_iv(&cipher_ctx, IV, 16);
```

Notice that now we have to store the IV in the cipher_context struct.

After this the rest of the program is identical. The IV is used to encrypt the first block and then after that mbedtls automatically uses the cipher text block to XOR with the current plain text. You can start the process over using the IV again by calling the mbedtls_cipher_reset function which you can think of as starting the chain of blocks.

To decrypt the blocks you have to process them in the order that they were created and you need the IV used to start the chain off:

```
char plaintext[16];
ret = mbedtls_cipher_setkey(&cipher_ctx, key,
                        cipher_info->key_bitlen, MBEDTLS_DECRYPT);
printf("%d",ret);
ret = mbedtls_cipher_set_iv(&cipher_ctx, IV, 16);
ret = mbedtls_cipher_reset(&cipher_ctx);
ret = mbedtls_cipher_update(&cipher_ctx, output, 16,
                                        plaintext, &olen);
printf("plain text %.16s\n", plaintext);
```

There is no need to worry about padding when using CBC mode as mbedtls will add bytes to make the block up to full size.

You can see the full modified program on the book's page at www.iopress.info.

If you try the program you will see the plain text and cipher text displayed as before. What you don't see is that if you used the program to encrypt Tux then the result would look like random noise and you have successfully hidden the patterns in the blocks.

Notice that as each block depends on the previous block you cannot parallelize the encryption. However, as each block is XORed with the cipher text of the previous block you can parallelize decryption and to decrypt a block all you need is the previous encrypted block and the key.

CTR, CCM, and GCM Modes

There are a great many variations on how block ciphers are applied to data, their so-called modes. As well as CBC, it is worth knowing about CTR, CCM, and GCM modes as these are commonly encountered.

CTR, CounTeR, mode seems to turn the encryption on its head. It takes a reproducible sequence of numbers and encrypts these rather than the plain text. The final cipher text is generated by XORing the plain text with the encrypted sequence. This is a form of "one-time pad" and it is provably secure as long as the sequence is kept secure. Of course, in this case the sequence is usually generated by a simple algorithm and hence it is possible for it to be discovered. To make this less likely, an IV is used to make the encryption more secure. The IV is appended to the counter, encrypted and XORed with the plain text. To decrypt the cipher text all you need is the IV and the key and, of course, knowledge of how the counter sequence was generated. Surprisingly most CTR modes use a sequential block count, i.e. 0, 1, 2, 3 and so on. The argument is that any weakness that this might create is a problem with the encryption algorithm, not the regular sequence used, as the encryption is supposed to mask any regularities in the plain text.

There are two other modes in common use and they improve over CBC and CTR by making it possible to authenticate the data. Using AES in ECB or CBC provides security, but it does nothing to authenticate the data. If any transmission errors occur, or if an attacker changes the data, the blocks will still decrypt without any indication of a problem, but the recovered plain text will be incorrect.

The obvious solution is to include a hash of the plain text in the cipher text and use this to detect any modifications to the data. There are many possible ways of doing this, but the two most commonly encountered are CCM and GCM.

CCM, Counter with cipher block Chaining Message, authentication is a modification of CTR mode. First a Message Authentication Code (MAC) is computed, specifically a CBC-MAC. This works by starting with an IV of zero and performing the usual CBC algorithm, i.e. XOR the IV with the plain text and then encrypt, use the resulting cipher text as the IV for the next block. The MAC is the final block. You can see that this is usable as a MAC as it depends in a complex way on all of the plain text. After this the plain text and the MAC are encrypted using CTR mode. The cipher text can be decrypted using CTR mode with the key and IV and the plain text can be checked by computing the MAC and comparing it to the original. CCM is used in IEEE 802.11 as part of WPA2, IPSec VPN, TLS 1.2 and BLE. It is also used in the Zigbee standard with extensions.

The final mode to be described, GCM, Galois Counter Mode, is based on similar ideas. It uses CTR mode for encryption, but the MAC is computed using a sophisticated hash function based on a polynomial field which is beyond the scope of this book. However, you can make use of GCM with mbedtls without needing to understand the mathematics as AES GCM is one of the available options. GCM is used in IEEE 802.1, IPSec VPN, SSH, TLS 1.2 and 1.3.

What Encryption Methods

There are lots of other functions to explore but using them to implement any cryptographic task follows the same general lines as the AES encryption example given earlier. For example, computing a hash value is very similar to implementing AES encryption but calling functions which are specific to hashing.

One useful technique is to find out what encryption types are supported:

```
const mbedtls_cipher_info_t *cipher_info;
const int *list;
printf("Available ciphers:\n");
list = mbedtls_cipher_list();
while (*list)
{
    cipher_info = mbedtls_cipher_info_from_type(*list);
    printf("  %s\n", cipher_info->name);
    list++;
}
```

A typical output from this is:

```
Available ciphers:
 AES-128-ECB
 AES-192-ECB
 AES-256-ECB
 AES-128-CBC
 AES-192-CBC
 AES-256-CBC
 AES-128-CCM
 AES-192-CCM
 AES-256-CCM
```

The Password Problem

The simplest method of ensuring that a user has the authority to make a change to the way a program works is to ask them to set a password during initialization and then to supply the password to get permission to make a change. The problem is that, to validate the password, you have to store it as part of the program and this means that the password is essentially public knowledge. Anyone with access to the device would find it comparatively easy to reverse engineer the code and find the password.

The solution to the problem is to not store the password at all. The usual approach is to compute a hash of the password. A hash function is a function that accepts data as its input and outputs a fixed size value that summarizes the data:

```
h = hash(data)
```

As the data is generally much larger than the hash, the value cannot be unique and it has to be possible that different data give the same hash – this is called a collision. A good hash function can be used to detect if changes have been made to the data without a detailed examination. If the data has changed the hash value will be different.

A good hash function has the smallest number of collisions and collisions should show no patterns that allow a user to work out a collision given a hash. That is, if:

```
h1 = hash(data1)
```

then a good hash function will make it very difficult to find a data2 that has the same hash:

```
h1 = hash(data2)
```

Given a suitable hash function we can now implement password protection without storing a password. What we do is compute a hash when the password is set and save that instead. When the user presents the password we again compute the hash and compare it to the stored hash. If the password is correct then the hash values will match. Of course, the hash value can now be found by an attacker, but this doesn't matter as much as the attacker now has to present not the hash but the password that produces the hash. As long as it is very difficult to find a collision with the given hash value, the system is secure against the hash value becoming public.

This is the case for hash functions such as SHA-256 and they can be used to implement password protection. To make it very secure you have to implement it with care. In particular, to avoid brute force attacks, you have to use a "salt" value – a random string which is concatenated with the password before the hash is computed:

```
h=hash(password+salt)
```

The salt is randomly generated for each password and stored along with the hash:

```
h,salt
```

That is, with salt the same password produces different hash values each time it is used. This prevents the construction of hash lookup tables for common passwords.

When it comes to password protection the details matter.

Summary

- A good source of random numbers is a key component of practical cryptography.

- Pseudo random number generators create numbers that "look" random in the sense that it is difficult to predict the next number without knowledge of the way they are generated.

- Hardware random number generators try to make use of apparent physical randomness to produce numbers that are difficult to predict.

- A third category of random number generators are the cryptographic generators which are essentially pseudo random number generators but with a proof that the sequence cannot be predicted in a reasonable time, even if you know the details of the generator.

- Hardware generators are the best choice for small machines but they usually suffer from not being perfectly random for a range of reasons. Hardware generators can be improved using randomness extractors.

- The Pico's ROSC is a good potential source of randomness but it has correlations that need to be removed by reading it infrequently and using a randomness extractor to pass NIST tests. The Pico SDK 1.5 introduces a set of random functions that pass the NIST tests.

- Any TLS connection involves a negotiation about which set of cryptographic methods, a cryptographic suite, to use.

- A particular suite is generally written as a list in the order
    `Key exchange-Authentication-Encryption method-Hash`

- Encryption methods can be added to the configuration header file of the mbedtls library.

- As well as implementing TLS, you can also use mbedtls for a range of different cryptographic tasks such as symmetric key encryption without the need to implement key exchange.

- AES encryption is a block encryption method and there are range of sub-methods concerning how the blocks are chained together to make the entire text secure.

- Passwords should never be stored. Instead a password hash with salt should be used.

The only difference between a server and a client is the ability to accept a connection. A client actively seeks a connection with a server, but a server has to just sit waiting patiently for a client to connect. The server also has the problem of having to deal with the possibility of having to deal with more than one client at a time and hence multiple simultaneous connections. The basics are the same - only the way server allows clients to connect is different.

If you are also going to create a secure server with TLS support then there is another difference. A client doesn't need a certificate, but a server does. When a client connects the server has to provide its certificate to the client to allow it to set up encrypted data exchange and to verify the server's identity. This means we need to know how to create and use a certificate if we are going to create a server.

As we already know how to use the Application Layered Module for adding TLS and making other modifications, it makes sense to carry on using it. There are, however, raw TCP functions corresponding to each of the altcp_ functions we use in this chapter. If you don't want to support TLS you could just use the raw TCP functions, but the efficiency gains are small.

A Basic TCP Server

A server is set up in exactly the same way as a client. You need to use altcp_new to create a PCB Protocol Control Block and fill it in with the appropriate callbacks:

```
struct altcp_pcb *pcb = altcp_new(NULL);
```

What the callbacks are will be explained later.

A difference is that you have to bind a server to particular network ports and a single machine might have more than one:

```
err_t altcp_bind(struct altcp_pcb *pcb,
                        const ip_addr_t *ipaddr, u16_t port)
```

You can use bind with a client to limit the network connections and hence IP addresses it can use, but this usually isn't necessary as you generally don't care what IP address a client has. You do generally care what IP address a server has because the client has to know it to connect. The binding is to a particular IP address and port number. As usual, you can use the IP address 0.0.0.0 to mean "any".

At this point the PCB is bound to the IP address and you could use altcp_connect to connect to a server as we have done in previous chapters. However, for a server we don't connect to anything - we simply listen for incoming connections:

```
cyw43_arch_lwip_begin();
pcb=altcp_listen(pcb);
cyw43_arch_lwip_end();
```

The altcp_listen function returns a new PCB which uses less memory than the original one, which is deallocated.

What is going to happen if a client tries to connect while the server is listening? The answer is that a new callback, accept, is called to deal with the connection. You can set the callback in the PCB in the usual way:

```
altcp_accept(pcb,accept);
```

and accept has to have the signature:

```
err_t accept(void *arg, struct altcp_pcb *pcb, err_t err);
```

As before the arg parameter is a custom parameter passed to all callbacks. What is different is that the pcb parameter is a brand new PCB that you can use to work with the connection to the client. That is, it isn't the PCB that you used to listen on. A new PCB is created for each client and the accept function has to add callbacks that will deal with client events, for example:

```
static err_t accept(void *arg, struct altcp_pcb  *pcb, err_t err)
{
    altcp_recv(pcb,recv);
    printf("connect!\n");
    return ERR_OK;
}
```

The recv callback deals with the data, i.e. the request that the client has sent to the server. This needs to be examined and then the altcp_write function is used to send the response back to the client.

Putting this together setting up the server is just a matter of:

```
struct altcp_pcb *pcb = altcp_new(NULL);
altcp_accept(pcb,accept);
altcp_bind(pcb,  IP_ADDR_ANY, 80);
cyw43_arch_lwip_begin();
pcb=altcp_listen(pcb);
cyw43_arch_lwip_end();
while (true)
{
    sleep_ms(500);
}
```

The simplest accept function is:

```
static err_t accept(void *arg, struct altcp_pcb  *pcb, err_t err)
{
    altcp_recv(pcb,recv);
    return ERR_OK;
}
```

and the recv function is the same as used in previous examples:

```
err_t recv(void *arg, struct altcp_pcb *pcb,
                                     struct pbuf *p, err_t err)
{
 if (p != NULL)
 {
 printf("recv total %d  this buffer %d next %d err %d\n",
                             p->tot_len, p->len, p->next, err);
 pbuf_copy_partial(p, myBuff, p->tot_len, 0);
 myBuff[p->tot_len] = 0;
 printf("Buffer= %s\n", myBuff);
 altcp_recved(pcb, p->tot_len);
 pbuf_free(p);
 }
 return ERR_OK;
}
```

The Response

If you try this out and connect to the Pico using a browser you will see something like:

```
Buffer= GET / HTTP/1.1
Host: 192.168.11.164
Connection: keep-alive
Cache-Control: max-age=0
Upgrade-Insecure-Requests: 1
User-Agent: Mozilla/5.0 (Windows NT 10.0; Win64; x64) AppleWebKit/537.36 (KHTML, like Gecko)
Chrome/109.0.0.0 Safari/537.36
Accept: text/html,application/xhtml+xml,application/xml;q=0.9,
            image/avif,image/webp,image/apng,*/*;q=0.8,application/signed-exchange;v=b3;q=9
Accept-Encoding: gzip, deflate
Accept-Language: en-GB,en-US;q=0.9,en;q=0.8,es;q=0.7
```

You have to parse at least the first line to discover that the request, in this case is a GET and the file required is the default. In this case we are going to send the same HTML file, no matter what the client asked for.

The HTML is easy enough:

```
char html[] =
"<html><head><title>Temperature</title></head>
 <body>
 {\"humidity\":81%, \"airtemperature\":23.5C}</p>
 </body>
 </html>\r\n";
```

This is a typical small page for a small server reporting back temperature and humidity. The HTML could be anything, as long as it is not too big. If this was real data from a sensor then the temperature and humidity would be dynamically added to the HTML string after reading. Also notice that the data takes the form of a JSON data object. In this case the JSON is wrapped by some simple HTML so that it can be displayed, but it is easy enough to change this so that we are transmitting raw JSON ready for processing, see later.

To send this HTML we need some HTTP headers defining what we are sending back. The simplest set of headers that work is something like:

```
HTTP/1.1 200 OK
Content-Type: text/html; charset=UTF-8
Server:Picow
Date: Sat, 13 Jun 2020  6:23:15 GMT
Content-Length:113
```

Notice that we now have two headers, `Date` and `Content-Length`, that need to be generated dynamically and be set to the current date and the size of the data portion respectively. There is also a blank line to mark the end of the headers. If you drop back to HTTP 1.0 you can avoid the dynamic headers, but they aren't difficult to construct.

It is easier to make the headers after you have created the HTML and know its length. The `Status` and `Content-Type` headers are static:

```
char headers[1024] = {0};
char Status[] = "HTTP/1.1 200 OK\r\nContent-Type: text/html;
                       charset=UTF-8\r\nServer:Picow\r\n";
```

Date and Time

We have a small problem with the date header, however, as the Pico doesn't have a Real Time Clock (RTC), that is set automatically or battery-backed up. Later we will look at using SNTP, Simple Network Time Protocol, to set the real time clock, but for now we will simply initialize it to a convenient date and convert it into a standard C tm struct.

It is unfortunate that the `RTC` `datetime_t` struct isn't organized to be compatible with the C `tm` struct which is supported by many useful date and time functions. However, it is fairly easy to convert between the two and this allows us to use standard C functions.

It is fairly easy to create a temporary initialization function:

```
void setRTC()
{
 datetime_t t = {
 .year = 2023,
 .month = 02,
 .day = 03,
 .dotw = 5,
 .hour = 11,
 .min = 10,
 .sec = 00};
 rtc_init();
 rtc_set_datetime(&t);
}
```

This needs to be called when the program starts to set the RTC which will then run and keep the current time until the program is restarted. To allow us to use the standard C date and time functions we can write a function that converts an RTC datetime_t struct into a tm struct:

```
void getDateNow(struct tm *t)
{
    datetime_t rtc;
    rtc_get_datetime(&rtc);

    t->tm_sec = rtc.sec;
    t->tm_min = rtc.min;
    t->tm_hour = rtc.hour;
    t->tm_mday = rtc.day;
    t->tm_mon = rtc.month - 1;
    t->tm_year = rtc.year - 1900;
    t->tm_wday = rtc.dotw;
    t->tm_yday = 0;
    t->tm_isdst = -1;
}
```

Notice that the yday, the number of days since the start of the year, isn't filled in correctly. This isn't important as we don't make use of it, but you can easily add an expression to compute it.

To use the RTC you have to change the target_link_libraries in the CmakeLists.txt file to read:

```
target_link_libraries(main pico_stdlib
     pico_cyw43_arch_lwip_threadsafe_background hardware_rtc)
```

i.e. add hardware_rtc. We also need to add:

```
#include "hardware/rtc.h"
```

With these two functions we can now construct a `Date` header:

```
struct tm t;
getDateNow(&t);
char Date[100];
strftime(Date, sizeof(Date),
                "Date: %a, %d %b %Y %k:%M:%S %Z\r\n", &t);
```

Content Length

Finally the `Content-Length` header can be constructed using the same technique:

```
char ContLen[100] = {0};
snprintf(ContLen, sizeof ContLen,
                "Content-Length:%d \r\n", strlen(html));
```

Finally we put all the headers together into a single string.

```
snprintf(headers, sizeof headers,
                "%s%s%s\r\n", Status, Date, ContLen);
```

Now we can assemble the data ready to be sent to the client:

```
char data[2048] = {0};
snprintf(data, sizeof data, "%s %s", headers, html);
```

sendData

Putting all this together into a function gives:

```
void sendData(struct altcp_pcb *pcb)
{
 err_t err;
 char html[] = "<html><head><title>Temperature</title></head>
             <body><p>{\"humidity\":81%,\"airtemperature\":23.5C}
                  </p></body></html>\r\n";
 char headers[1024] = {0};
 char Status[] = "HTTP/1.1 200 OK\r\nContent-Type:
                  text/html;charset=UTF-8\r\nServer:Picow\r\n";
 struct tm t;
 getDateNow(&t);
 char Date[100];
 strftime(Date, sizeof(Date),
                    "Date: %a, %d %b %Y %k:%M:%S %Z\r\n", &t);
 char ContLen[100] = {0};
 snprintf(ContLen, sizeof ContLen,
                    "Content-Length:%d \r\n", strlen(html));
 snprintf(headers, sizeof headers, "%s%s%s\r\n",
                                      Status, Date, ContLen);
 char data[2048] = {0};
 snprintf(data, sizeof data, "%s%s", headers, html);
 err = altcp_write(pcb, data, strlen(data), 0);
 err = altcp_output(pcb);
}
```

This function can be called from the recv callback handler to respond to the client:

```
err_t recv(void *arg, struct altcp_pcb *pcb,
                                   struct pbuf *p, err_t err)
{
 char myBuff[BUF_SIZE];
 if (p != NULL)
   {
      printf("recv total %d  this buffer %d next %d err %d\n",
                         p->tot_len, p->len, p->next, err);
      pbuf_copy_partial(p, myBuff, p->tot_len, 0);
      myBuff[p->tot_len] = 0;
      printf("Buffer= %s\n", myBuff);
      altcp_recved(pcb, p->tot_len);
      pbuf_free(p);
      sendData(pcb);
   }
    return ERR_OK;
}
```

Managing Connections

If you put all this together then you will find that it works, but there are some rough edges to the way it behaves. In particular, it can't handle more than one or at most two requests at a time. It also does nothing about closing connections. Of the two, closing connections is the more complicated. The problem is that HTTP 1.1 expects the connection to be kept open for more requests. This is complicated and the simplest solution is to close the connection as soon as the server has finished with it. The easiest place to do this is in the sent callback:

```
static err_t sent(void *arg, struct altcp_pcb *pcb, u16_t len)
{
    altcp_close(pcb);
}
static err_t accept(void *arg, struct altcp_pcb *pcb, err_t err)
{
    altcp_recv(pcb, recv);
    altcp_sent(pcb, sent);
    printf("connect!\n");
    return ERR_OK;
}
```

The only problem with this is that it might also kill any additional requests that the client has made on the same connection. How important this is depends on the data you are trying to transfer and on the way the client handles the abrupt disconnection. Notice that even with this modification the server will still deal with two requests from a general browser – one for the data and one for the site's icon which it responds to by sending the data again.

If you want the server to deal with multiple requests on a single connection then your only choice is to use the `poll` callback to close a connection after it has been idle for the specified time:

```
static err_t poll(void *arg, struct altcp_pcb *pcb){
        printf("Connection Closed");
        altcp_close(pcb);
}

altcp_poll(pcb, poll,10);
```

Of course, if you choose to leave connections open until they have been idle for a long time, you are more likely to need to handle multiple connections. As lwIP isn't being used in a multithreaded environment this has to be done using a queue. There are two additional versions of the `listen` function:

```
struct altcp_pcb* altcp_listen_with_backlog(struct altcp_pcb  *pcb,
                                              u8_t backlog)
```

and:

```
struct altcp_pcb* altcp_listen_with_backlog_and_err(
                struct altcp_pcb *pcb, u8_t backlog, err_t *err)
```

In practice, the first two listen functions are implemented as macros that call `altcp_listen_with_backlog_and_err` with defaults for the remaining parameters. The `backlog` parameter sets the size of the queue and the `err` parameter returns an error code if the `listen` returns `NULL`.

To allow this to work you also need:

```
#define TCP_LISTEN_BACKLOG      1
```

in your `lwipopts.h`.

For example, changing the listen function to:

```
pcb = altcp_listen_with_backlog(pcb,3);
```

allows for three connection attempts to be queued. In practice you may not notice the difference if you are trying to connect with a browser as these use various retry algorithms that cover up an inability to connect at once.

A Simple Server

The complete C program is:

```
#include <stdio.h>
#include "pico/stdlib.h"
#include "pico/cyw43_arch.h"
#include "lwip/pbuf.h"
#include "lwip/altcp_tcp.h"
#include "hardware/rtc.h"
#include "time.h"
#include "setupWifi.h"
```

```c
#define BUF_SIZE 2048

void getDateNow(struct tm *t)
{
    datetime_t rtc;
    rtc_get_datetime(&rtc);

    t->tm_sec = rtc.sec;
    t->tm_min = rtc.min;
    t->tm_hour = rtc.hour;
    t->tm_mday = rtc.day;
    t->tm_mon = rtc.month - 1;
    t->tm_year = rtc.year - 1900;
    t->tm_wday = rtc.dotw;
    t->tm_yday = 0;
    t->tm_isdst = -1;
}

void sendData(struct altcp_pcb *pcb)
{
    err_t err;
    char html[] = "<html><head><title>Temperature</title></head>
        <body><p>{\"humidity\":81%,\"airtemperature\":23.5C}
        </p></body></html>\r\n";
    char headers[1024] = {0};
    char Status[] = "HTTP/1.1 200 OK\r\n
                    Content-Type: text/html;charset=UTF-8\r\n
                    Server:Picow\r\n";

    struct tm t;
    getDateNow(&t);
    char Date[100];
    strftime(Date, sizeof(Date),
                    "Date: %a, %d %b %Y %k:%M:%S %Z\r\n", &t);
    char ContLen[100] = {0};
    snprintf(ContLen, sizeof ContLen, "Content-Length:%d \r\n",
                                                strlen(html));
    snprintf(headers, sizeof headers, "%s%s%s\r\n",
                                            Status, Date, ContLen);
    char data[2048] = {0};
    snprintf(data, sizeof data, "%s%s", headers, html);
    err = altcp_write(pcb, data, strlen(data), 0);
    err = altcp_output(pcb);
}
```

```c
err_t recv(void *arg, struct altcp_pcb *pcb,
                                    struct pbuf *p, err_t err)
{
    char myBuff[BUF_SIZE];
    if (p != NULL)
    {
        printf("recv total %d  this buffer %d next %d err %d\n",
                        p->tot_len, p->len, p->next, err);
        pbuf_copy_partial(p, myBuff, p->tot_len, 0);
        myBuff[p->tot_len] = 0;
        printf("Buffer= %s\n", myBuff);
        altcp_recved(pcb, p->tot_len);
        pbuf_free(p);
        sendData(pcb);
    }
    return ERR_OK;
}

static err_t sent(void *arg, struct altcp_pcb *pcb, u16_t len)
{
    altcp_close(pcb);
}

static err_t accept(void *arg, struct altcp_pcb *pcb, err_t err)
{
    altcp_recv(pcb, recv);
    altcp_sent(pcb, sent);
    printf("connect!\n");
    return ERR_OK;
}

void setRTC()
{
    datetime_t t = {
        .year = 2023,
        .month = 02,
        .day = 03,
        .dotw = 5,
        .hour = 11,
        .min = 10,
        .sec = 00};
    rtc_init();
    rtc_set_datetime(&t);
}
```

```
int main()
{
    stdio_init_all();
    setRTC();
    connect();

    struct altcp_pcb *pcb = altcp_new(NULL);
    altcp_accept(pcb, accept);
    altcp_bind(pcb, IP_ADDR_ANY, 80);
    cyw43_arch_lwip_begin();
    pcb = altcp_listen_with_backlog(pcb,3);
    cyw43_arch_lwip_end();
    while (true)
    {
        sleep_ms(500);
    }
}
```

You also need to change the target_link_libraries in the CmakeLists.txt file to read:

```
target_link_libraries(main pico_stdlib
pico_cyw43_arch_lwip_threadsafe_background hardware_rtc)
```

i.e. add hardware_rtc.

And for the backlog queue to work you need to add:

```
#define TCP_LISTEN_BACKLOG       1
```

in your lwipopts.h.

A Polling Server

If you followed the discussion of implementing an HTTP client you might well expect the conversion of the callback-driven server into a polling mode so that everything can be done in the main polling loop. In fact, servers really suit the callback model of execution much better than the client. The reason is that the client decides what is to happen and in what order and in the client this has to be integrated into everything else that it does – flash leds, take sensor readings etc. What this means is that the client is best implemented along the general lines of:

```
while (true)
{
    get data to be sent to server;
    put data to server;
    do other things;
}
```

For a server, however, it is still the client that determines what will happen and in this case its operation is something like:

```
accept(){
    send current data to client;
}

while (true)
{
    get data to be sent to server;
    do other things;
}
```

In other words, the main polling loop can spend its time flashing lights and reading sensors as long as it stores the data somewhere that the callback can access it. When the client connects, the callback interrupts the main polling loop and sends the current data to the client.

You can see that, in a very general way, polling suits the client while callbacks suit the server.

It is clear that the server can't do much work in the callback as this stalls the server and the WiFi stack in general. Callbacks need to be short and to complete in as short a time as possible.

There is a subtle point to note in this approach. The polling loop communicates with the callbacks via shared global variables. Clearly this poses a race hazard in that the callback can interrupt an update and so send spurious data to the client. The solution is to surround any update of shared variables with cyw43_arch_lwip_begin() and cyw43_arch_lwip_end() which disable the interrupt and hence act like a lock for the update.

As with the callback the locking should be for as short a time as possible:

```
t=getReadingFromSensor();
cyw43_arch_lwip_begin();
temperature=t;
cyw43_arch_lwip_end();
```

It is probably better to use the new async contexts introduced in SDK 1.5 for locking:

```
t=getReadingFromSensor();
async_context_acquire_lock_blocking(cyw43_async_context);
temperature=t;
async_context_release_lock(cyw43_async_context);
```

where it is assumed that getReadingFromSensor might take many milliseconds to complete and the temperature variable is global and accessed by the callback to send the data to the client. The lock ensures that the update of the temperature variable is never interrupted by a client request.

Certificates

If you want to implement an SSL server then things are slightly more complicated because you need to provide a certificate. Getting a certificate can be an involved process. Even popular, free, certificate-issuing sites like Let's Encrypt require proof that you own the domain that the certificate applies to. To do this you have to write code which generates a new key pair and then either create a specific DNS record or store a file on the website. This is easy enough for production purposes, but not so easy when you are in the process of creating a program.

The usual solution is to create a self-signed certificate. If the operating system has OpenSSL installed, and Windows and most versions of Linux do, then you can create a key and certificate pair using:

```
openssl req -newkey rsa:2048 -nodes -keyout iopress.key -x509
                                    -days 365 -out iopress.crt
```

changing *iopress* to the name of your server. You will be asked a set of questions for information that is included in the certificate. How you answer these questions only modifies what the user sees if they ask to inspect the certificate so you can simply accept the defaults. The only exception to this is the common name prompt. This needs to match the name of the server that the certificate is intended for. It has to correspond to the server name returned in the server header.

The openssl command creates two files, a .key file and a .crt file, which need to be processed to create strings that can be used in the Pico program. Normally the files would be loaded into the server, but the Pico doesn't support a standard filing system and so the binary in the files needs to be loaded into a pair of strings. The certificate and key are saved on disk using an encoding called Base64 with a line of unencoded ASCII text at the start and end. To make use of this data we have to remove the first and last line of the file and un-encode the Base64 to a standard byte or ASCII string.

This can be done using standard operating system command line programs, but it is also very easy to write a standard Python program to do the job:

```python
import binascii

with open("iopress.key", 'rb') as f:
    lines = f.readlines()
lines = b"".join(lines[1:-1])
key = binascii.a2b_base64(lines)

res = ""

for b in key:
    res += "0x%02x," % b

res="u8_t key[]={"+res[:-1]+"};"
print(res)

with open("iopress.crt", 'rb') as f:
    lines = f.readlines()
lines = b"".join(lines[1:-1])
cert = binascii.a2b_base64(lines)
res = ""
for b in cert:
    res += "0x%02x," % b

res="u8_t cert[]={"+res[:-1]+"};"
print()
print(res)
```

If you run this program, with the names of the .key and .crt files corrected to apply to the certificate you have generated, then it will read in each file, remove the first and last line, remove the Base64 encoding and print the C line needed to load the file's contents into an array:

```
u8_t key[] = {0x30, 0x82, 0x04, 0xbd, 0x02, … };
u8_t cert[] = {0x30, 0x82, 0x03, 0x9b, 0x30, … };
```

where the long list of hex codes has been truncated to save space.

You can simply copy and paste these two lines to get the certificate you have generated into the program. Once we have the certificates in the program the rest is fairly straightforward.

Adding HTTPS

As we have used `altcp` to build our simple server it is easy to convert it to HTTPS. The only real difference from the client is that we need to use `altcp_tls_create_config_server_privkey_cert` to create the `ltcp_tls_config` struct:

```
struct altcp_tls_config *tls_config=
        altcp_tls_create_config_server_privkey_cert(
            privkey,privkey_len,privkey_pass,privkey_pass_len,
                                              cert,cert_len);
```

If the key isn't password protected you can pass `NULL` and 0 for those parameters.

The conversion to TLS simply involves replacing the line:

```
struct altcp_pcb *pcb = altcp_new(NULL);
```

with:

```
u8_t key[] = {0x30, 0x82, 0x04,  . . .};
u8_t cert[] = {0x30, 0x82, 0x03,  . . .};

struct altcp_tls_config *tls_config =
        altcp_tls_create_config_server_privkey_cert(
                    key, sizeof(key), NULL, 0, cert, sizeof(cert));
struct altcp_pcb *pcb = altcp_tls_new(tls_config, IPADDR_TYPE_ANY);
```

To work with standard HTTPS you have to listen on port 443:

```
altcp_accept(pcb, accept);
altcp_bind(pcb, IP_ADDR_ANY, 443);
```

You also need to add:

```
#include "lwip/altcp_tls.h"
```

From this point on the program is the same, but now works with a TLS connection.

You also have to add:

```
#define MBEDTLS_SSL_SRV_C
```

to `mbedtls_config.h` to activate the server TLS protocol. As this is a server it is also worth including elliptic curve cryptography and GCM AES mode.

The `CmakeLists.txt` target_link_libraries line has to be modified to read:

```
target_link_libraries(main pico_stdlib
pico_cyw43_arch_lwip_threadsafe_background hardware_rtc
pico_lwip_mbedtls pico_mbedtls)
```

i.e we now need `lwip_mbedtls` and `pico_mbedtls`.

The modifications to the simple HTTPS server are simple, but you can find the complete listing on the book's page at www.iopress.info.

If you try this out and look at the output of the serial port you will notice that when a browser tries to connect using https://*ip address* there are a number of

```
mbedtls_ssl_handshake failed: -30592
```

messages. These refer to attempts that have been made to negotiate a cryptographic suite that isn't supported by the server. If you want to see fewer of them, increase the number of key exchange and encryption methods you support.

When the handshake finally works the browser will warn you that the certificate isn't valid. The following is what you will see if you use Chrome.

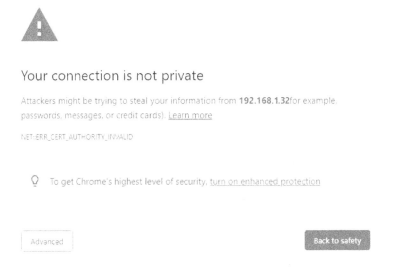

Messages like this are because browsers don't trust self-signed certificates. However, if you allow the page to download it will use SSL encryption. To do this click on Advanced and then confirm that you want to proceed. You can force a browser to accept the certificate by adding it to its trusted root certification authorities tab. However, for most testing purposes this isn't necessary. If you have a valid certificate and key for a particular web server you can substitute it for the self-signed certificates.

It is worth saying that making an SSL connection is not fast. The Pico is being asked to do significant computation to implement the cryptography and the handshake process is involved and hence time-consuming. You will also see a number of exceptions caused by the client aborting the connection due to the self-signed certificate, which is perfectly normal. Firefox is a much more friendly browser to use when testing SSL connections. Chrome tends to want to lock things down as soon as it detects a problem with the certificate.

If you are seeing error messages about running out of memory then perform a hard reset on the Pico. The problem is that any SSL sockets that are not closed when the program ends due to an exception survive a soft reset and so slowly use up memory. A hard reset solves the problem.

Notice that this is a secure server in the sense that the connection is encrypted, but as the certificate is self-signed there is no way to authenticate the server. Anyone else can create a certificate and pretend to be you. In addition to this problem there is the issue of physical access to the Pico. Not only is your public key contained in the certificate, the private key is hex encoded for everyone to see. If an attacker can physically access the Pico then there is no way you can stop them from reading, and hence using, your private key. How much of a problem this is depends on what else the key is used for. Do not reuse a private key that is used to secure SSH connections or other servers as part of a Pico-based server unless the device is physically secure.

A Practical Web Server

You can continue to elaborate on the server's architecture and its capabilities, but building a reasonably functional web server is difficult and time consuming. For simple tasks, such as sending a small amount of sensor data or receiving configuration commands, the raw approach described above is workable and results in more efficient code. However, for anything complicated it is better to use the web server application included in lwIP as the HTTP server module.

The only problem with the approach is keeping the size of the executable small. The reason that this is a problem is that the website the server is associated with is compiled into the executable. As long as the website is just a few pages with minimal graphics there should be no problems.

To get a web server started is trivial:

```
#include <stdio.h>
#include "pico/stdlib.h"
#include "pico/cyw43_arch.h"
#include "lwip/apps/httpd.h"
#include "setupWifi.h"

int main()
{
    stdio_init_all();
    connect();
    httpd_init();
    while (true)
    {
        sleep_ms(500);
    }
}
```

The CmakeLists.txt file has to have pico_lwip_http added to the target_link_libraries and you need the standard lwipopts.h file with:

```
#undef TCP_WND
#define TCP_WND    16384
#define LWIP_ALTCP              1
#define LWIP_DEBUG 1
#define TCP_LISTEN_BACKLOG 1
```

added to the end.

The single function call:

```
httpd_init();
```

starts the server running and at this point you can use a web browser on another machine to connect to its IP address and you will see the default website compiled into the program:

SICS lwIP - A Lightweight TCP/IP Stack

The web page you are watching was served by a simple web server running on top of the lightweight TCP/IP stack lwIP.

lwIP is an open source implementation of the TCP/IP protocol suite that was originally written by Adam Dunkels of the Swedish Institute of Computer Science but now is being actively developed by a team of developers distributed world-wide. Since it's release, lwIP has spurred a lot of interest and has been ported to several platforms and operating systems. lwIP can be used either with or without an underlying OS.

The focus of the lwIP TCP/IP implementation is to reduce the RAM usage while still having a full scale TCP. This makes lwIP suitable for use in embedded systems with tens of kilobytes of free RAM and room for around 40 kilobytes of code ROM.

More information about lwIP can be found at the lwIP homepage at http://savannah.nongnu.org/projects/lwip or at the lwIP wiki at http://lwip.wikia.com .

If you don't see it try a clean rebuild of all projects.

Creating a web server really is this easy on the Pico with the help of lwIP. However, if you want to customize the website that is served we still have some work to do. The question to be answered is where does the webpage come from?

A Custom Website

The Pico doesn't have a file system that can be used to install a website. In Linux and Windows machines web servers work by accepting requests from clients to download a particular file by simply finding the file in the file system and downloading it. You can see that for the Pico, and most other small machines, this isn't possible. The solution adopted by lwIP is to use a utility program that will convert a website stored in the machine's file system into a single C file that can be compiled into the program that is using the server.

The reason that the previous example worked is that a demo website is included with the library in `pico/pico-sdk/lib/lwip/src/apps/http`. The file that stores the default website is called `fsdata.c` and this is automatically included in your program when you build it.

Clearly to create a custom website we are going to have to convert a set of HTML files and graphics into a new `fsdata.c`. The program that does this is supplied as part of the lwIP library, but only in source form. To make use of it you have to compile it and this can be tricky. If you would rather download a pre-compiled version you can do so from the I Programmer website, www.i-programmer.info. Navigate to the Code Bin where you will find a version for the Raspberry Pi and one for Windows.

If you want to build your own copy this is reasonably easy using VS Code. Open the folder at:

`pico/pico-sdk/lib/lwip/src/apps/http/makefsdata`

Create a `CmakeFiles.txt` containing:

```
cmake_minimum_required(VERSION 3.13)
project(makefsdata C CXX ASM)
set(CMAKE_C_STANDARD 11)
set(CMAKE_CXX_STANDARD 17)
add_executable(htmlgen
 makefsdata.c
)
target_include_directories(htmlgen
        PRIVATE ../../../../src/include/
        PRIVATE ../../../../contrib/ports/unix/port/include/
        PRIVATE ${CMAKE_CURRENT_LIST_DIR})
```

For Windows change the line:

PRIVATE ../../../../contrib/ports/unix/port/include/

to:

PRIVATE ../../../../contrib/ports/win32/include/

Notice that the name of the executable changes to htmlgen, which is the name that the help documentation uses.

Also add a copy of lwipopts.h to the directory – the default one from examples will do. Next use the command Configure CMake and on the Pi select the kit GCC 10.2.1 arm-linux-gnueabihf or a later version.

Under Windows select Visual Studio Build Tools 2019 Release – x86.

In both cases there are the compilers for the machines that the utility will run on, i.e. not the Pico. Next build the program. There is no need to configure debugging or Run commands.

When the build finishes you will find htmlgen in the build directory. Copy the executable to:

pico/pico-sdk/lib/lwip/src/apps/http

If you run it in this directory it will read the files in the fs subdirectory and convert them into fsdata.c. You can find out more about the utility by running it from the command line with the parameter –help:

```
makefsdata v2.2.0d - HTML to C source converter
    by Jim Pettinato          - circa 2003
    extended by Simon Goldschmidt  - 2009

Usage: htmlgen [targetdir] [-s] [-e] [-11] [-nossi] [-ssi:<filename>] [-c] [-f:<filename>] [-m]
[-svr:<name>] [-x:<ext_list>] [-xc:<ext_list>

  targetdir: relative or absolute path to files to convert
  switch -s: toggle processing of subdirectories (default is on)
  switch -e: exclude HTTP header from file (header is created at runtime, default is off)
  switch -11: include HTTP 1.1 header (1.0 is default)
  switch -nossi: no support for SSI (cannot calculate Content-Length for SSI)
  switch -ssi: ssi filename (ssi support controlled by file list, not by extension)
  switch -c: precalculate checksums for all pages (default is off)
  switch -f: target filename (default is "fsdata.c")
  switch -m: include "Last-Modified" header based on file time
  switch -svr: server identifier sent in HTTP response header ('Server' field)
  switch -x: comma separated list of extensions of files to exclude (e.g., -x:json,txt)
  switch -xc: comma separated list of extensions of files to not compress (e.g., -xc:mp3,jpg)
  if targetdir not specified, htmlgen will attempt to
  process files in subdirectory 'fs'
```

By default the utility converts everything in the fs directory and its sub-directories and it creates static headers for all of the "files" it creates in fsdata.c. This, of course, creates a static website that is fast to serve, but not very flexible. To overcome this problem the web server allows both CGI and SSI, Server Side Includes, see below.

To make use of htmlgen, copy it into your project directory and create a directory called fs. You can put into this folder any webpage files and resources, including a sub-folder structure, and htmlgen will automatically convert everything into a single C file. To try things out, create index.html in the fs folder containing:

```
<html>
<head>
    <title>My First Page</title>
</head>
<body>
    <p>Hello Pico web Server World!</p>
</body>
</html>
```

Next run htmlgen and you should see fsdata.c appear in the same folder as htmlgen. Rename fsdata.c to myfs.c. Now add the line:

```
#define HTTPD_FSDATA_FILE "myfs.c"
```

to the lwipopts.h. This tells the server the name and where to find the fs file. You can include a path as well as a file name, but in this case it is in the project folder so it will be found with a relative path.

To try this out you will need to perform a complete clean rebuild – the fact that the fs file has changed is often missed by CMake. As long as you do a clean build, you should see the new website when you open it in a browser. If you don't and still see the default you haven't done a clean rebuild or you haven't changed the name of fsdata.c and added the line to the lwipopts.h file.

From this point you can build webpages as complicated as you like. They can include images, but the image files have to be in the fs directory or a sub-directory. You can even include JavaScript in the page and it too will be converted into data within the fs file. You need to remember that every time you change the website stored in the fs directory you need to do a clean rebuild.

By default htmlgen adds a standard set of headers to the fs file. This is simple but it means you cannot create dynamic webpages – see later to find out how to do this.

You can customize the way that htmlgen creates the fs file and the headers in particular by adding defines to the lwipopts.h in its own directory. Don't confuse this lwipopts.h file with the one in the server applications directory that controls how the server is built. The one in /lib/lwip/src/apps/http controls how htmlgen constructed the fs file that the server will supply to the clients. For example, to compile in a specific server name to the headers you can add:

```
#define HTTPD_SERVER_AGENT "Picow"
```

to the end of lwipopts.h.

Adding HTTPS to the Server App

The web server application is built using `altcp` and as a result it is very easy to convert it to HTTPS. All we have to do is use `httpd_inits()` in place of `httpd_init()` and pass it a struct `altcp_tls_config` suitably initialized with key and certificate. That is you replace:

```
httpd_init();
```

in the main program by:

```
u8_t key[] = {0x30, 0x82, 0x04, 0xbd, . . . };
u8_t cert[] = {0x30, 0x82, 0x03, 0x6b, . . .};
struct altcp_tls_config *tls_config =
          altcp_tls_create_config_server_privkey_cert(
                          key, sizeof(key),
                               NULL, 0, cert,sizeof(cert));
httpd_inits(tls_config);
```

To make this work you also need to make some changes to `lwipopts.h`. To enable the HTTPS code you need to add:

```
#define HTTPD_ENABLE_HTTPS    1
```

You also need to change the server name that is sent as part of the headers. As the headers are compiled into `fsdata.c` you need to add:

```
#define HTTPD_SERVER_AGENT "PicoW"
```

to the `lwipopts.h` file in the `lwip/src/apps/http/makefsdata/` folder and you need to recompile the website using `htmlgen`.

If you now compile and run the program you can connect using HTTPS, but if you are still using the supplied test webpages you will find that a browser cannot connect. The reason is that HTTPS/TLS needs more memory and the index page is too large to process. The solution is to add:

```
#undef MEM_SIZE
#define MEM_SIZE                      8000
```

to `lwipopts.h`. If you need to serve even larger pages you may need to increase the memory allocated to lwIP. Note that to make this work you need to do a clean rebuild.

A Dynamic Web Page – Server Side Includes

The web server we have so far makes it very easy to serve a static website, but for data-collection purposes typically a device like the Pico needs a dynamic webpage where measurements can be displayed. For example, if you have a temperature and humidity sensor connected to the Pico then you probably would like a webpage that displays the current temperature and humidity. This isn't possible with a static webpage because all of the details of the page are compiled into the `fsdata.c` file by the `htmlgen` utility at build time and making changes at run time isn't easy.

The solution is to use SSI, Server Side Includes. The idea is simple. A tag of the form:

`<!--#name-->`

where *name* is the name of the tag you are to replace with data when the page is downloaded, is included in the HTML. The server looks for SSI tags within files with the extensions .shtml, .shtm, .ssi, .xml or .json. When it finds a tag it calls the `SSIHandler` that you have set up and it can insert some text into the page before it is sent to the client.

An `SSIHandler` is passed different parameters depending on how things are set up, but the default is:

`u16_t mySSIHandler(int iIndex, char *pcInsert, int iInsertLen)`

The `iIndex` parameter gives the index of the SSI tag that has been found. The `pcInsert` parameter is a pointer to a buffer that you can use to store the text you want inserted following the SSI tag. The `iInsertLen` gives the maximum number of characters you can insert, 192K by default.

To register the SSIHandler we have to use:

```
http_set_ssi_handler(tSSIHandler ssi_handler,
                     const char **tags,
                     int num_tags)
```

The first parameter is the handler, the second is an array of strings specifying the names of the tags and the third specifies the number of tags, i.e. the size of the array.

For example, to introduce two tags temp and hum and insert values for each before the page is served:

```
const char *ssitags[] = {"temp", "hum"};

u16_t mySSIHandler(int iIndex, char *pcInsert, int iInsertLen)
{
    switch(iIndex){
        case 0:
            snprintf(pcInsert, iInsertLen, "42 C");
            break;
        case 1:
            snprintf(pcInsert, iInsertLen, "80%%");
            break;
    }
}
```

Of course, in a real application you would insert strings that were derived from sensors, not dummy test values. The HTML page has to be modified to read:

```
<html>
  <head>
    <title>Test Page</title>
  </head>
  <body>
    <p>
Hello Pico W Server World <br/>
The Temperature is: <!--#temp--><br/>
The Humidity is: <!--#hum--><br/>
    </p>
  </body>
</html>
```

and should be saved as Index.ssi.

The main program is now:

```
    http_set_ssi_handler(mySSIHandler, ssitags, 2);
    httpd_init();

    while (true)
    {
        sleep_ms(500);
    }
```

Notice the http_set_ssi_handler call before starting the server.

If you want to work with HTTPS then change the main program to:

```
u8_t key[] = {0x30, 0x82, 0x04, 0xbd, . . .};
u8_t cert[] = {0x30, 0x82, 0x03, 0x6b, . . . };
struct altcp_tls_config *tls_config =
        altcp_tls_create_config_server_privkey_cert(
          key, sizeof(key), NULL, 0, cert, sizeof(cert));

http_set_ssi_handler(mySSIHandler, ssitags, 2);
httpd_inits(tls_config);
while (true)
{
    sleep_ms(500);
}
```

We also need to add:

`#define LWIP_HTTPD_SSI    1`

to `lwipopts.h`. This enables testing for SSI tags.

Now when you run the program and use a browser to navigate to:

`http://IP/index.ssi`

or

`https://IP/index.ssi`

as long as you are working with TLS you should see:

← → C   ⚠ Not secure | 192.168.253.46/index.ssi

🌐 New Tab

Hello Pico W Server World
The Temperature is: 42 C
The Humidity is: 80%

or:

← → C   ⚠ Not secure | https://192.168.11.164/index.ssi

🌐 New Tab

Hello Pico W Server World
The Temperature is: 42 C
The Humidity is: 80%

147

Using SSI tags is the simplest and most useful way of creating dynamic webpages using the lwIP web server.

If you look at the HTML sent to the client you will find that the SSI tags are still present. If you want them removed add:

```
#define LWIP_HTTPD_SSI_INCLUDE_TAG 0
```

to `lwipopts.h`.

Many useful configuration defines can be added to `lwipopts.h`. For example:

```
#define LWIP_HTTPD_MAX_TAG_INSERT_LEN 192
```

sets the maximum number of characters you can insert in an SSI tag and:

```
#define HTTPD_SERVER_AGENT "lwIP/" LWIP_VERSION_STRING "
                    (http://savannah.nongnu.org/projects/lwip)"
```

sets the server identity sent to the client in the headers.

One confusing factor is that sometimes you have to modify the `lwipopts.h` file in your project and in the one used to build `htmlgen`. For example, if you want to extend SSI to standard HTML pages you need to include the line:

```
#define LWIP_HTTPD_SSI_EXTENSIONS ".shtml", ".shtm", ".ssi",
                                ".xml", ".json",".html"
```

in `lwipopts.h` in the project and in `htmlgen`. The reason is that `htmlgen` has to avoid adding a header for the content size to SSI files because it can't know the final size of the page. You then need to rebuild `htmlgen` and use it to create the `fsdata.c` to be used with the project. Of course, you can edit the `#define` to be any list of file extensions you care to treat as SSI.

Listing

The complete server program using TLS is:

```c
#include <stdio.h>
#include "pico/stdlib.h"
#include "pico/cyw43_arch.h"
#include "lwip/altcp_tls.h"
#include "lwip/apps/httpd.h"
#include "hardware/structs/rosc.h"
#include "hardware/rtc.h"
#include "time.h"
#include "setupWifi.h"

#define BUF_SIZE 2048

void getDateNow(struct tm *t)
{
    datetime_t rtc;
    rtc_get_datetime(&rtc);

    t->tm_sec = rtc.sec;
    t->tm_min = rtc.min;
    t->tm_hour = rtc.hour;
    t->tm_mday = rtc.day;
    t->tm_mon = rtc.month - 1;
    t->tm_year = rtc.year - 1900;
    t->tm_wday = rtc.dotw;
    t->tm_yday = 0;
    t->tm_isdst = -1;
}

void setRTC()
{
    datetime_t t = {
        .year = 2023,
        .month = 02,
        .day = 05,
        .dotw = 0,
        .hour = 6,
        .min = 14,
        .sec = 00};
    rtc_init();
    rtc_set_datetime(&t);
}

const char *ssitags[] = {"temp", "hum"};
```

```c
u16_t mySSIHandler(int iIndex, char *pcInsert, int iInsertLen)
{
    switch(iIndex){
        case 0:
            snprintf(pcInsert, iInsertLen, "42 C");
            break;
        case 1:
            snprintf(pcInsert, iInsertLen, "80%%");
            break;
    }
}

int main()
{
    stdio_init_all();
    setRTC();
    connect();


    u8_t key[] = {0x30, 0x82, 0x04, 0xbd, ...};
    u8_t cert[] = {0x30, 0x82, 0x03, 0x6b, ... };
    struct altcp_tls_config *tls_config =
        altcp_tls_create_config_server_privkey_cert(
                  key, sizeof(key), NULL, 0, cert, sizeof(cert));

    http_set_ssi_handler(mySSIHandler, ssitags, 2);
    httpd_inits(tls_config);
    while (true)
    {
        sleep_ms(500);
    }
}
```

The SSI demonstration file is:

```
<html>
 <head>
 <title>Test Page</title>
 </head>
 <body>
 <p>
Hello Pico W Server World <br/>
The Temperature is: <!--#temp--><br/>
The Humidity is: <!--#hum--><br/>
 </p>
   </body>
</html>
```

The CmakeLists.txt file is:

```
cmake_minimum_required(VERSION 3.13)
set(PICO_BOARD pico_w)
set(CMAKE_C_STANDARD 11)
set(CMAKE_CXX_STANDARD 17)

include(pico_sdk_import.cmake)
project(PicoW C CXX ASM)
pico_sdk_init()

add_executable(main
 main.c
)

target_include_directories(main PRIVATE ${CMAKE_CURRENT_LIST_DIR}
                    /home/pi/pico/pico-sdk/lib/mbedtls/include)

target_link_libraries(main pico_stdlib
                pico_cyw43_arch_lwip_threadsafe_background
                    hardware_rtc pico_lwip_mbedtls
                            pico_mbedtls pico_lwip_http)
pico_add_extra_outputs(main)
```

The extra lines in the lwipopts.h file are:

```
#undef TCP_WND
#define TCP_WND  16384

#define LWIP_ALTCP              1
#define LWIP_ALTCP_TLS          1
#define LWIP_ALTCP_TLS_MBEDTLS  1

#define LWIP_DEBUG 1
#define ALTCP_MBEDTLS_DEBUG  LWIP_DBG_ON
#define TCP_LISTEN_BACKLOG          1


#define HTTPD_ENABLE_HTTPS   1
#undef MEM_SIZE
#define MEM_SIZE                 8000
#define LWIP_HTTPD_SSI   1
```

DIY or pico_lwip_http

Creating a server, HTTP or HTTPS isn't difficult, unless you have to cover a range of interactions with the client. If all you want to do is send a simple webpage with minimal customization then the DIY approach will result in a simpler program and a more secure program as you can hard code its behavior. For example, the server can be set to ignore all but the requests you want to service.

If you need to support a range of different interactions and complex webpages then using the supplied HTTP app has advantages. As well as supporting SSI, it also supports a simplified CGI with parameters supplied by a GET and it implements a simple POST interaction.

However, all of this said, it is worth repeating the advice that running a client to transfer data to a server via a PUT or a POST using HTTPS is much more secure as there is no need to have a certificate in the client.

Summary

- The only difference between a server and a client is the ability to accept a connection. A client actively seeks a connection with a server, but a server has to just sit waiting patiently for a client to connect.

- A server has to listen on a specified IP/Port and when a client tries to connect it has to accept the connection. Each client opens a new TCP connection in addition to the one used for listening.

- HTTP needs the date and time to be set to supply information for the date header.

- We also need to work out the number of bytes in the response and use this to set the Content-Length header.

- Polling isn't an appropriate approach to implementing a server, which is inherently asynchronous. Callbacks need to be kept short as they block the handing of other clients.

- To extend the HTTP server to HTTPS we need to include a certificate as a string of bytes.

- In most cases a self-signed certificate can be created using OPENSSL and used for testing.

- The lwIP library includes a server module which supports a range of more advanced features including SSI, Server Side Includes.

- To use the server module you have to compile the HTML pages you want to serve into a C program using the htmlgen utility.

- The server module can also implement HTTPS using altcp.

The UDP (User Datagram) protocol is very different from the more usual TCP (Transmission Control Protocol) connection. UDP is very basic. There is no error correction and no guarantee that datagrams, i.e. packets, will arrive in the order they were sent. All you get is a checksum error detection mechanism that lets you detect any corruption in the data the datagram is carrying. Using IPv4 the data in a datagram is limited to 65,507 bytes, but this limit can be exceeded using IPv6. UDP can also broadcast datagrams simultaneously to as many clients as care to receive them.

After this description you may be wondering why anyone would consider using UDP in preference to TCP. The simple answer is speed. There are few overheads to UDP and it is ideal for sending fast packets of data, as long as packet loss and order don't matter or can be engineered to not matter. It is the basis for a number of other fast simple protocols such as DHCP (Dynamic Host Configuration Protocol), DNS (Domain Name System) and NTP (Network Time Protocol) and is used in audio and video applications to implement streams of data.

Basic UDP

A UDP packet is very simple. The usual IP header is used and its payload is a UDP datagram. This has a 32-bit header which has the format:

bytes	
0, 1	Source port number
2, 3	Destination port number
4, 5	Length of data payload including header
6, 7	Checksum

The source port number and checksum are optional and often set to zero and ignored. The length gives the total length of the payload including the header and hence has to be 8 or larger. The largest packet that can be sent is set by the use of a 16-bit value but it is actually smaller than you might expect due to the need to accommodate the IP header.

For IPv4 the largest UDP packet is 65,507 bytes. The checksum field holds a checksum for all of the data, the header and the IP header and it is used for optional error checking.

There are a range of standard port numbers that are used for particular tasks as is the case for TCP. For example, port 123 is used for SNTP and should be avoided for other purposes. Ports above 49152 are not standardized and can be used for anything. Of course, you still have to avoid collisions between different applications. One approach is to use a random assignment of port numbers with the server informing the client of the port in use by some other standard protocol.

UDP Server

A UDP server sends datagrams to another machine specified by IP address and port number. The other machine has to be ready to receive UDP packets, if not the packets are just lost as there is no checking that they have been correctly delivered. In this sense a UDP server isn't really a server as it doesn't allow a client to connect in any sense and it is simply a source of packets.

The basic operation of raw UDP is the same as for TCP. There is a PCB, Protocol Control Bock, that you have to initialize and there are functions to set the PCB up and to send and receive datagrams.

To create a UDP PCB we use:

```
struct udp_pcb *pcb = udp_new();
```

This has to be bound to an IP address and a port and these are used to determine which network interface is used to send the datagram. You can use IP_ADDR_ANY to use any available interface:

```
udp_bind(pcb, IP_ADDR_ANY, 8080);
```

The port used, 8080, isn't typically used for UDP, but it has a higher probability of working through firewalls. If this program doesn't work on a particular machine then it is almost certain that it is a firewall rule that is blocking it or the lack of a rule to allow it. If you specify a 0 for port it will automatically bind to a random port between UDP_LOCAL_PORT_RANGE_START and UDP_LOCAL_PORT_RANGE_END.

There are a number of ways of specifying the destination address, but storing it in the PCB follows the method that TCP uses:

```
ip_addr_t ip;
IP4_ADDR(&ip, 192, 168, 11, 101);
udp_connect(pcb,&ip,8080);
```

This doesn't cause anything to happen on the network. It simply stores the information in the PCB. Notice that the remote port doesn't have to be the same as the source port. If the remote machine needs to send datagrams back then, by default, it will either use the source port if specified or the remote port otherwise. There is a `disconnect` function:

```
udp_disconnect(pcb)
```

but all this does is to zero the fields in the PCB – there is no sense in which a UDP client and server are connected they simply exchange datagrams.

To send data we need to use a PBUF of the correct type and size and store the data in its `payload` field:

```
char message[] = "Hello UDP World";
struct pbuf *p = pbuf_alloc(PBUF_TRANSPORT,
                            strlen(message)+1, PBUF_RAM);
snprintf(p->payload, strlen(message)+1, "%s", message);
```

There are many ways of transferring the data into the payload field but using snprint has the advantage of being able to incorporate data from different sources.

Finally we can send the datagram:

```
err_t er = udp_send(pcb, p);
pbuf_free(p);
```

Notice that we have to free the PBUF and you cannot reuse it to send another payload as it has been replaced by the UDP packet that has been sent.

The complete program is:

```
#include <stdio.h>
#include "pico/stdlib.h"
#include "pico/cyw43_arch.h"
#include "lwip/pbuf.h"
#include "lwip/udp.h"
#include "setupWifi.h"
int main()
{
    stdio_init_all();
    connect();
    struct udp_pcb *pcb = udp_new();
    udp_bind(pcb, IP_ADDR_ANY, 8080);
    ip_addr_t ip;
    IP4_ADDR(&ip, 192, 168, 11, 101);
    udp_connect(pcb, &ip, 8080);
    char message[] = "Hello UDP World";
    struct pbuf *p = pbuf_alloc(PBUF_TRANSPORT,
                        strlen(message) + 1, PBUF_RAM);
    snprintf(p->payload, strlen(message) + 1, "%s", message);
    err_t er = udp_send(pcb, p);
    pbuf_free(p);
    while (true)
    {
        sleep_ms(500);
    }
}
```

The `lwipopts.h` and `CmakeLists.txt` file are the very simplest. The define:

```
#define LWIP_UDP        1
```

has to be included in `lwipopts.h` for the UDP library to be compiled but this is in the default `lwipopts.h` file from the Pico examples.

There is also a

```
udp_sendto(pcb,p,ip,port)
```

function which can be used to send a packet to the machine specified by `ip` and `port` without making any changes to the PCB.

There is one special use of UDP, DHCP (Dynamic Host Configuration Protocol), which requires sending a datagram to a machine even though the current network connection doesn't yet have an IP address of its own. To do this you can use the two special functions:

```
udp_sendto_if(pcb,p,dst_ip,dst_port,netif)
```

and

```
udp_sendto_if_src(pcb,p,dst_ip,dst_port,netif, src_ip)
```

These send a datagram to the destination `ip` and `port` number using the `netif` interface. The second function also includes the specified source `ip` address in the datagram even though the interface might not have an IP address yet.

Notice that you can have multiple PCBs active at any given time and can use any of them to send a UDP packet to a given IP address and port. The PCBs are managed in a linked list and you can use:

```
udp_remove(pcb)
```

to remove, and hence effectively deactivate and free, the `pcb`.

A Python UDP Client

It can be difficult to test UDP programs without a suitable client or server to connect to. Using Python it is very easy to create a UDP client which can be used to test UDP servers:

```python
import asyncio
class ClientDatagramProtocol(asyncio.DatagramProtocol):
    def datagram_received(self, data, addr):
        message = data.decode("utf8")
        print("Received",message,"from", addr)
```

```
async def main():
    loop = asyncio.get_running_loop()
    transport, protocol = await loop.create_datagram_endpoint(
            lambda: ClientDatagramProtocol(),
                    local_addr=('0.0.0.0', 8080))
    await asyncio.sleep(100000)
    transport.close()

asyncio.run(main())
```

If you want to know more this program is from *Programmer's Python: Async* by Mike James, ISBN: 978-1871962595.

UDPLite

Usually a datagram includes a checksum computed on all of the data including the header. If the receiving client computes the checksum and it doesn't agree with the value included in the datagram then the whole packet is discarded and the application knows nothing about the server's attempt to send a packet. Often this is exactly what is required. Usually the client has some method of deciding when a datagram has gone missing. For example, a sequence number and a timeout can be used to trigger a request that the server send the datagram again. More often the loss of a datagram is simply tolerated.

For some applications, however, the use of a checksum is too sensitive. The whole datagram is discarded if even a single bit is in error. If the error is confined to a small number of bits and can be tolerated then a better option is to use UDPLite, which restricts the calculation of the checksum to a given number of bytes. The header always has to be in the checksum because if there was even a single-bit error in it then the datagram might not even be intended for the recipient.

To set UDPLite mode you need to add:

```
#define LWIP_UDPLITE 1
```

to the `lwipopts.h` configuration file.

You also need to set the number of bytes included in the checksum for received or transmitted packets:

```
pcb→chksum_len_tx = n;
pcb→chksum_len_rx = n;
```

If you set n to 8 then only the header is checked. Notice that you have to set UDPLite on both ends of the connection. If you send an UDPLite datagram to a client that is expecting a standard datagram or is checking a different number of bytes then the datagram will be discarded as being in error.

Broadcast UDP

You can use UDP to send a datagram to all of the machines on the network. Whether this is a good idea or not is debatable. IPv6 has abandoned broadcast UDP in favor of multicasting, which is just as simple from the program's point of view, but requires the network to be set up to use it and a router or managed switch that supports it. In short, broadcasting is simple, but not supported by IPv6.

You can set the server given earlier to broadcast with just a one small change:

```
IP4_ADDR(&ip, 192, 168, 11, 255);
udp_connect(pcb, &ip, 8080);
```

The IP address has to be in the same sub-net, i.e. 192.168.11.x in this case, but the final octet has to be 255. Nothing else has to change and the UDP client works as it did, but now any machine running it on the same sub-net will receive the datagram.

Usually you have to enable broadcast UDP for it to work, but the lwIP UDP module has it enabled by default.

A UDP Client

The obvious thing to do is to write a client that can receive the datagram sent by the previous example or by the Python server given below. Many examples of using UDP do so on a single machine, passing the datagram between two programs via the local loopback connection. This usually works, but it doesn't make clear the distinction between client and server. In this case it is assumed that the client is running on a different machine that is reachable by the server running on another machine.

As is the case for TCP reception of data, you have to use the PCB to set up a callback when there is data to be processed:

```
struct udp_pcb *pcb = udp_new();
udp_recv(pcb, recv, NULL);
```

This simply sets the appropriate field in the PCB. To start listening for packets you have to bind the PCB to an IP address and port number:

```
udp_bind(pcb, IP_ADDR_ANY, 8080);
```

From this point on any datagrams received by the network interface with the correct port number which causes the `recv` callback to be activated. Notice that this works no matter where the packet originated from. Of course, the server can send a broadcast packet and it will be received by all of the clients listening on that port. There can be more than one PCB active at any

160

given time and all of the IP addresses and ports that they define will be received. To "close" a UDP PCB, i.e. to stop responding to its IP and port address, you have to use the:

```
udp_remove(pcb)
```

function.

The recv callback is much the same as the recv function that we use with TCP. The data is provided in a PBUF struct:

```
void recv(void *arg, struct udp_pcb *pcb, struct pbuf *p, const
ip_addr_t *addr, u16_t port)
{
    char myBuff[BUF_SIZE];
    if (p != NULL)
    {
        printf("recv total %d  this buffer %d next %d \n",
                            p->tot_len, p->len, p->next);
        printf("From %s:%d\n",ipaddr_ntoa(addr),port);
        pbuf_copy_partial(p, myBuff, p->tot_len, 0);
        myBuff[p->tot_len] = 0;
        printf("Buffer= %s\n", myBuff);
        pbuf_free(p);
    }
}
```

Notice that the IP address and port of the sender is provided in the callback parameters. The documentation warns that the IP address might be a pointer into the PBUF and hence not valid after it has been freed. If you have multiple PCBs using the same recv callback you can use the IP address and port to work out what sort of UDP packet has been received.

If you run this particular client on the machine with the correct IP address and a server, either the previous server on a Pico or the Python server given in the next section, when the server sends a datagram you will see:

```
recv total 15  this buffer 15 next 0
From 192.168.11.101:8080
Buffer= Hello UDP World
```

There is no limit on the number of datagrams that can be received. If you don't see the message when both client and server are running then the only possible reasons are that you are using the wrong IP address on the server or, and this is more likely, the firewall on the client is stopping the datagrams arriving.

If you want to narrow down the servers that can send data to the client you can connect the PCB to a remote IP address and a port number:

```
IP4_ADDR(&ip, 192, 168, 11, 101);
udp_connect(pcb, &ip, 8080)
```

After this only UDP packets from 192.168.11.101 on port 8080 will be received by the client.

A Custom Python UDP Server

While you can use another Pico to send UDP packets to a client, it is useful to have a Python program that can run on almost anything:

```
import asyncio

async def main():
    loop = asyncio.get_running_loop()
    transport, protocol = await loop.create_datagram_endpoint(
                            lambda: asyncio.DatagramProtocol(),
                            local_addr=('0.0.0.0',8080))

    data=b"Hello UDP World"
    for i in range(20):
        transport.sendto(data,addr=("192.168.11.168",8080))
        await asyncio.sleep(1)
    transport.close()

asyncio.run(main())
```

This sends twenty packets at one second intervals to the specified IP address. Again it is from *Programmer's Python: Async*, ISBN: 978-1871962595.

Polling UDP

There is no reason to make any special provision for sending UDP packets as there is no need to wait for a connection to be made. You can incorporate a UDP send into the main polling loop in your program without any problems:

```
setup PCB
while(true){
      get sensor readings
      store sensor readings in PBUF
      send(PCB,PBUF)
      free PBUF
      do more work
}
```

Of course, receiving a UDP packet is asynchronous and hence callback-driven and so much more difficult to work into a polling loop. This is another example of the "output is easy – input is hard" meme – output is easy because you decide when to do it and input is hard because external agents determine when you need to do it.

To convert a UDP receive event into something suitable for polling all we need is a flag to indicate when there is something to do. For example:

```
int dataReady=false

recv(){
        copy packet data to buffer
        dataready=true
}


while(true){
        if(data ready){
                process data
                dataready=false
        }
        do more work
}
```

In practice things are a little more complicated than this because you have to allow for the fact that another packet may be received while you are processing an existing packet – you need to implement a queue.

Summary

- UDP is a lightweight protocol that can be used to exchange data between two machines.

- The sending machine specifies the address of the receiving machine and a port number.

- The receiving machine specifies the address and port number it wants to receive data from.

- UDP doesn't offer error correction or confirmation of receipt. Essentially packets or datagrams are sent into the network for other machines to pick up and if they are lost on the way that's something that has to be accommodated.

- There is error detection in the form of a checksum. Any datagram that has an error is automatically discarded.

- Implementing a UDP client or server follows the same lines as the use of TCP.

- There is a UDPLite protocol which allows you to ignore any errors in the data detected by the checksum.

- Datagrams can be broadcast to every machine on the local network but only using IPv4.

Chapter 8

SNTP For Time-Keeping

SNTP, Simple Network Time Protocol, is a network protocol for obtaining an accurate time and date and it is the obvious way to set the Pico W's Real Time Clock (RTC) without the need for additional hardware or user intervention. Knowing the correct time and date is particularly important if you are using certificates as these have to be checked to ensure they are still valid and not expired.

A full SNTP client is quite complicated and lwIP supplies a basic implementation as an application. However, for the purposes of setting the Pico's RTC we can use a much simpler approach.

SNTP is an extensive topic of which we'll only cover a small fraction. You can find out about it in detail at https://www.ntp.org/.

Unicast SNTP

There are two versions of SNTP, Multicast and Unicast.

The Multicast protocol broadcasts time packets that anyone can pick up and is useful for keeping a local network synchronized. The Unicast protocol is slightly more complicated from the client's point of view in that it has to request a packet, but it is the norm on the wider Internet.

To make use of SNTP we have to use UDP as described in the previous chapter.

The basic transaction is simple.

1. The client sends an SNTP data structure as UDP packet using port 123 to the server.

2. The server then sends an SNTP data structure as a UDP packet back using the same port to the client.

The Structure of Time

The key to using SNTP is the SNTP data structure which consists of four 32-bit words followed by four 64-bit timestamps. There is also an optional 96-bit authenticator, which can be used to verify the server's identity, but this isn't used by publicly available time servers.

◄───── 4 bytes ─────►

| Command and Information |
| Root delay |
| Root dispersion |
| Reference identifier |
| Reference time stamp |
| Originate time stamp |
| Receive time stamp |
| Transmit time stamp |

SNTP time packet

Each of the time stamps uses the same 64-bit format.

- The first 32 bits comprise an unsigned binary integer that gives the number of seconds since the so-called "fiducial date" - midnight on January 1, 1900.

- The next 32 bits is a pure binary fraction giving the fractional part of the seconds since the fiducial date.

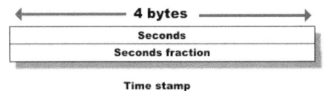

◄───── 4 bytes ─────►

| Seconds |
| Seconds fraction |

Time stamp

Time Stamp format

The time stamp is always expressed using Universal Time (UT) and converting it to your local time zone is left to the client.

Interestingly there is a problem contained in this time stamp format that is very similar to the Millennium Bug, aka Year 2000 problem. Currently the high bit of the time stamp is set and it is heading to roll over in 2036, hence the "Y2036 bug problem".

SNTPv4, the latest version, appears to introduce a standard which uses a 128-bit date format: 64 bits for the second and 64 bits for the fractional-second. This has enough range to work until the end of the universe or 585 billion years.

However, this isn't quite what it seems as even SNTPv4 uses the usual 64-bit format to send the current time and it is left to the client to expand this to a full 128-bit date by determining the "era" via other means.

The prime epoch, i.e. 00h on 1 Jan 1900, corresponds to an era of zero, i.e. the high-order 64 bits are set to zero. Once the date passes 00h on 1 Jan 2036 the era will be set to one and the timestamp will roll over to zero. That is the full 128 bit date is given by

`128-bit date = era x` 2^{32} `+ timestamp`

and it is for the client to determine the value of `era` by other means.

Another way to look at this is that at the moment the timestamp measures the seconds from 00h on 1 Jan 1900 and after the rollover it measures seconds from 00h on 1 Jan 2036 and so on.

As SNTP is used to set the current date and time you can effectively ignore the problem and set the current date and time using the timestamp from the fiducial date that is appropriate for your era. Notice that this approach doesn't work for timestamps that are used to record when something happened as the era cannot be deduced in the same way.

The Time Commands

The first 32-bit word of the packet is an information and command word and from the specification it seems to be the only part of the structure you need to set before sending the request.

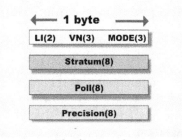

The first word

The first byte is most important. The first two bits carry leap second information and can mostly be ignored if you are only interested in setting the RTC to a reasonably accurate time:

LI	
00	No warning
01	Last minute has 61 seconds
10	Last minute has 59 seconds)
11	Alarm condition (clock not synchronized)

The next three bits, VN, specify the SNTP version and can be set to 3 or 4 by a client.

The final three bits specify what should happen, i.e. the state. MODE should be set to 3 for a client request and the server will set it to 4 in the response packet.

Mode	
0	Reserved
1	Symmetric active
2	Symmetric passive
3	Client
4	Server
5	Broadcast
6	Reserved for NTP control message
7	Reserved for private use

The remaining three bytes provide information on the server's time keeper. Stratum gives the level of time precision.

Stratum	
0	Unspecified or unavailable
1	Primary reference (e.g., radio clock)
2-255	Secondary reference (via NTP or SNTP)

Poll gives the minimum time between packets that the server can send. This is a signed integer giving the power nearest power of 2 in seconds. For example a value of 0 indicates 1 second, a value of 1 indicates 4 seconds, -1 indicates 1/2 second and so on.

Precision is an 8-bit signed integer giving the clock's precision, again as a power of 2 in seconds. The following three words are timestamps giving the root delay, i.e. the round trip delay to the server's primary time source; the root dispersion, i.e. the relative error of the server's time against the primary time source.

Reference identifier, i.e. a 4-byte ASCII code specifying the type of clock used as the standard.

The only problem with the reference identifier is that it isn't specified in the standard, but for stratum 1 servers you can look out for:

ATOM = Atomic clock
PPS   = Precision Pulse Source
GPS   = Global Positioning Satellite

and so on.

Radio clocks often quote their radio call sign. For a secondary reference the four bytes are often the TCP/IP address of the primary server.

The Timestamps

When you get the time packet back it contains four timestamps that can be used to improve the estimate of the current time:

- ◆ Reference Time Stamp (RefTS) – Time the server's clock was last set
- ◆ Transmit Time Stamp (TTS) - Time at the server when the packet left
- ◆ Originate Time Stamp (OTS) - Time you sent the request packet
- ◆ Receive Time Stamp (RTS) - Time the server received the packet.

These values can be used to estimate the round trip time and correct the final time to the last few tenths of a millisecond.

In practice you can ignore all of this unless you really are trying for high accuracy. All that matters is the TTS which contains the time as measured at the server when the packet was transmitted – this will be accurate to a few milliseconds unless the conditions on the Internet are so bad that you would be well advised to use an alternative server.

So it looks as if we can ignore all the time stamps in the requesting package and only look at the TTS value in the return package.

The only problem is that some servers ignore packets with unreasonable values of OTS in the requesting packet, but when making the first request there is no reasonable way to set this value.

Simple SNTP Client

As we only want to set the RTC we can greatly simplify the interaction with an SNTP server. You might think that the first thing we have to do is set up a struct suitable for holding the data, but there is no need as we are only interested in the first byte in the request packet and bytes 40-44 in the reply, which give the number of seconds from the fiducial date. Given this is all we want, direct access to the PBUF to set and get the data is sufficient.

First we need to set up a UDP connection on port 123, the standard SNTP port, to a suitable server. The first problem we have is determining which server to use. In principle you should never hard code the IP address of an SNTP server into a program. Instead you should allow DNS to select a suitable server from a pool of servers, but as this is a simple client we can start by hard coding an IP address which you can find from the ntp.org website:

```
struct udp_pcb *pcb = udp_new();
udp_recv(pcb, recv, NULL);
udp_bind(pcb, IP_ADDR_ANY, 123);
ip_addr_t ip;
IP4_ADDR(&ip, 128, 138, 140, 44);
udp_connect(pcb, &ip, 123);
```

The address used in this example is an NIST server and you should select a server close to you for an accurate result and to spread the load.

Next we set up a suitable request buffer:

```
struct pbuf *p = pbuf_alloc(PBUF_TRANSPORT, 48, PBUF_RAM);
uint8_t *payload = (uint8_t *)p->payload;
memset(payload, 0, 48);
*payload = 0x23;
err_t er = udp_send(pcb, p);
pbuf_free(p);
```

Notice that all we do is zero the 48-byte payload and then set the first byte to 0x23 which is version 4 and mode equals client. After sending the packet we can free the PBUF and wait for the callback to be called with the response.

The recv function is only interested in the four bytes starting at byte 40 in the 48-byte response:

```
void recv(void *arg, struct udp_pcb *pcb, struct pbuf *p, const
ip_addr_t *addr, u16_t port)
{
    if (p != NULL)
    {
        uint8_t seconds[4];
        pbuf_copy_partial(p, seconds, sizeof(seconds), 40);
        volatile uint32_t seconds_since_1900 =
            seconds[0] << 24 | seconds[1] << 16 |
                            seconds[2] << 8 | seconds[3];
        printf("time stamp %u", seconds_since_1900);
        pbuf_free(p);
        udp_remove(pcb);
    }
}
```

You can see that the contents of the PBUF are copied to the seconds array. The only complication is that the timestamp is in big endian format and the Pico uses little endian so we have to reverse the order of the bytes. At the end of the function we can not only free the PBUF but we can also remove the PCB so as not to receive and process any more UDP packets.

Setting the RTC

The Pico has a Real Time Clock, RTC, but without battery backup it has to be set each time the Pico starts. The obvious thing to do if you are working with a Pico W is to use SNTP to set the clock at the start of the program and perhaps at regular intervals while it is running. We already have the basic code to use an SNTP server to find the current timestamp, but as this is a more realistic application we cannot simply code the IP address of an SNTP server. Instead we have to use an IP address returned by one of the "pool servers". A pool server has a list of time servers that it issues in response to a DNS request so as to spread the load.

For example, if you query pool.ntp.org or time.nist.gov then a different SNTP server is returned each time on a round robin basis so that the load is spread between the servers in the pool. So we need to use Domain Name Service (DNS) to find a server. We also need to implement a polling approach to getting the time so that the main polling loop can continue to do something while waiting for the RTC to be set.

The basic flow of control is:

1. Use DNS to resolve an SNTP pool URL to a particular machine.
2. When we have the IP address the DNS callback starts a UDP request for the time.
3. When the time is ready the UDP recv callback has to process the data and set the RTC.

You can see that we have two callbacks to cope with and this distorts the logic of the program. As it is very likely that setting the RTC is going to be performed once at the start of the application and then perhaps once every few hours or so to correct the clock, it makes reasonable sense to implement it as a single task. We need a struct to record the status of the set RTC request:

```
struct timeStatus
{
    bool ready;
    struct udp_pcb *pcb;
};
```

We need the PCB so that we can cancel the UDP connection after a timeout. Of course you could add fields to retain more status information. The getSNTP function has to get the IP address of the SNTP server to be used and then hand control to the DNS callback:

```
struct timeStatus *getSNTP()
{
    struct timeStatus *tstatus = malloc(sizeof(struct timeStatus));
    tstatus->ready = false;
    tstatus->pcb=NULL;
    ip_addr_t ip;
    cyw43_arch_lwip_begin();
    err_t err = dns_gethostbyname("time.nist.gov",
                                      &ip, dns_found, tstatus);
    cyw43_arch_lwip_end();
    if (err == ERR_OK)
    {
        printf("DNS cache %s\n", ipaddr_ntoa(&ip));
        dns_found("", &ip, tstatus);
    }
    return tstatus;
}
```

If the DNS is found in the cache then dns_found is called synchronously otherwise it is called as a callback later. In both cases it gets the tstatus struct to modify. The getSNTP also returns the tstatus struct so that it can be tested by a polling function.

The next thing to happen is that the dns_found function is called and it has to make the SNTP UDP request:

```
void dns_found(const char *name, const ip_addr_t *ip, void *arg)
{
    struct timeStatus *tstatus = (struct timeStatus *)arg;
    printf("DNS %s\n", ipaddr_ntoa(ip));
    struct udp_pcb *pcb = udp_new();
    tstatus->pcb = pcb;
    udp_recv(pcb, recv, arg);
    udp_bind(pcb, IP_ADDR_ANY, 123);
    udp_connect(pcb, ip, 123);
    struct pbuf *p = pbuf_alloc(PBUF_TRANSPORT, 48, PBUF_RAM);
    uint8_t *payload = (uint8_t *)p->payload;
    memset(payload, 0, 48);
    *payload = 0x1b;
    err_t er = udp_send(pcb, p);
    pbuf_free(p);
}
```

This is very similar to the previous SNTP UDP request function. It sets up a PCB and sends the PBUF with the 48-byte payload requesting a time update. Notice that the PBUF is deallocated at the end of the function, but the PCB isn't and it is recorded in the tstatus struct which is passed to the recv callback.

The recv callback is the next function to be called and its job is to transfer the data in the received UDP packet into the RTC:

```
void recv(void *arg, struct udp_pcb *pcb, struct pbuf *p, const
ip_addr_t *addr, u16_t port)
{
 struct timeStatus *tstatus = (struct timeStatus *)arg;
 printf("SNTP responded\n");
 if (p != NULL)
 {
    uint8_t seconds_buf[4];
    pbuf_copy_partial(p, seconds_buf, sizeof(seconds_buf), 40);
    uint32_t seconds_since_1900 = seconds_buf[0] << 24 |
             seconds_buf[1] << 16 | seconds_buf[2] << 8 |
                                              seconds_buf[3];
    time_t seconds_since_1970 = seconds_since_1900 - 2208988800;
    struct tm *datetime = gmtime(&seconds_since_1970);
    setRTC(datetime);
    pbuf_free(p);
    udp_remove(pcb);
    tstatus->pcb=NULL;
    tstatus->ready = true;
 }
}
```

This follows much the same pattern as the previous function that decoded the timestamp. The one difference is that we convert the seconds_since_1900 that the SNTP server delivers into seconds_since_1970, which is what Unix/Linux, and hence the C library, uses. Once in a form suitable for using with C library functions, the timestamp is converted into a tm struct and then the setRTC function, which was given in Chapter 6 is used to set the date and time. Now that we have the date and time we can remove the UDP PCB and set the tstatus ready field to true to indicate that the task is complete.

If the SNTP server doesn't respond then the recv callback is never called and we need to cancel the operation after a timeout:

```
void cancelSNTP(struct timeStatus *tstatus)
{
    if (tstatus != NULL)
    {
        udp_remove(tstatus->pcb);
        free(tstatus);
        tstatus = NULL;
        printf("canceled\n");
    }
}
```

If tstatus is NULL then the operation has been completed and everything closed so there is nothing to cancel. Notice that this can be called at any time to cancel the operation.

Finally we need a polling function which can be used to check the status of the operation:

```
bool pollSNTP(struct timeStatus *tstatus)
{
    if (tstatus == NULL)
        return true;
    if (tstatus->ready)
    {
        free(tstatus);
        tstatus = NULL;
        return true;
    }
    return false;
}
```

This returns false when the process is still in progress and true when the connection has been closed. Notice that returning true doesn't mean that the RTC has been successfully updated only that the connection is closed for one reason or another.

If the RTC has been successfully updated, the getDateNow function will
return true and the date and time in a tm struct:

```
bool getDateNow(struct tm *t)
{
    datetime_t rtc;
    bool state = rtc_get_datetime(&rtc);
    if (state)
    {
        t->tm_sec = rtc.sec;
        t->tm_min = rtc.min;
        t->tm_hour = rtc.hour;
        t->tm_mday = rtc.day;
        t->tm_mon = rtc.month - 1;
        t->tm_year = rtc.year - 1900;
        t->tm_wday = rtc.dotw;
        t->tm_yday = 0;
        t->tm_isdst = -1;
    }
    return state;
}
```

This is just a small modification to the function given in Chapter 6. The
rtc_get_datetime function only returns true if the RTC has been initialized
and is running. Again we convert the Pico specific datetime_t struct to the
Linux/Unix tm struct. This allows us to use the standard C date/time
functions.

With all this in place we can now write a main program that makes use of it:

```
int main()
{
    stdio_init_all();
    connect();
    while (true)
    {
        struct timeStatus *tstatus = getSNTP();
        sleep_ms(500);
        if (pollSNTP(tstatus))
            break;
        cancelSNTP(tstatus);
    }
    while (true)
    {
        struct tm t;
        getDateNow(&t);
        char Date[100];
        strftime(Date, sizeof(Date),
                "Date: %a, %d %b %Y %k:%M:%S %Z\r\n", &t);
        printf("%s\n", Date);
        sleep_ms(5000);
    }
}
```

The first while loop starts the process of getting the date and time. If this hasn't completed in 500ms then the chances are that the server isn't responding or the packet has been lost. If this is the case then the operation is canceled and started over. Once the RTC has been set, the second while loop takes over and it simply prints the date and time every five seconds.

In a real program the first and second while loops could well be replaced by a single polling loop and another mechanism used to detect a timeout.

There are some problems with this program and with all lwIP SNTP-based applications. The problem is that the DNS requests are cached and there is no way to disable the cache. What is supposed to happen is that each time the pool URL is looked up a different server should be returned. The cache stops this happening. If the SNTP server you are using doesn't work then there is no way you can get an alternative because each time you look up the pool address the same server is returned from the cache. The only way to get an alternative SNTP server is to set the cache size to one entry by adding:

```
#define DNS_TABLE_SIZE 1
```

to lwipopts.h and then looking up another URL which resolves and is stored in the cache. The next time you look up the pool URL, it isn't returned from the cache and you should get a new server.

If you plan to use something like this program to set up the RTC then you need to add some error handling for the possibility that the DNS could fail.

The full program is:

```
#include <stdio.h>
#include "pico/stdlib.h"
#include "pico/cyw43_arch.h"
#include "lwip/pbuf.h"
#include "lwip/udp.h"
#include "setupWifi.h"
#include "hardware/rtc.h"
#include "time.h"
#include "lwip/dns.h"
```

```
bool getDateNow(struct tm *t)
{
 datetime_t rtc;
 bool state = rtc_get_datetime(&rtc);
    if (state)
    {
        t->tm_sec = rtc.sec;
        t->tm_min = rtc.min;
        t->tm_hour = rtc.hour;
        t->tm_mday = rtc.day;
        t->tm_mon = rtc.month - 1;
        t->tm_year = rtc.year - 1900;
        t->tm_wday = rtc.dotw;
        t->tm_yday = 0;
        t->tm_isdst = -1;
    }
    return state;
}

void setRTC(struct tm *datetime)
{
    datetime_t t;
    t.year = datetime->tm_year + 1900;
    t.month = datetime->tm_mon + 1;
    t.day = datetime->tm_mday;
    t.dotw = datetime->tm_wday;
    t.hour = datetime->tm_hour;
    t.min = datetime->tm_min;
    t.sec = datetime->tm_sec;
    rtc_init();
    rtc_set_datetime(&t);
}

struct timeStatus
{
    bool ready;
    struct udp_pcb *pcb;
};
```

```c
void recv(void *arg, struct udp_pcb *pcb, struct pbuf *p,
                            const ip_addr_t *addr, u16_t port)
{
    struct timeStatus *tstatus = (struct timeStatus *)arg;
    printf("SNTP responded\n");
    if (p != NULL)
    {
        uint8_t seconds_buf[4];
        pbuf_copy_partial(p, seconds_buf, sizeof(seconds_buf), 40);
        uint32_t seconds_since_1900 = seconds_buf[0] << 24 |
                seconds_buf[1] << 16 | seconds_buf[2] << 8 |
                                            seconds_buf[3];
        time_t seconds_since_1970 =
                                seconds_since_1900 - 2208988800;
        struct tm *datetime = gmtime(&seconds_since_1970);
        setRTC(datetime);
        pbuf_free(p);
        udp_remove(pcb);
        tstatus->pcb=NULL;
        tstatus->ready = true;
    }
}
bool pollSNTP(struct timeStatus *tstatus)
{
    if (tstatus == NULL)
        return true;
    if (tstatus->ready)
    {
        free(tstatus);
        tstatus = NULL;
        return true;
    }
    return false;
}
void dns_found(const char *name, const ip_addr_t *ip, void *arg)
{
    struct timeStatus *tstatus = (struct timeStatus *)arg;
    printf("DNS %s\n", ipaddr_ntoa(ip));
    struct udp_pcb *pcb = udp_new();
    tstatus->pcb = pcb;
    udp_recv(pcb, recv, arg);
    udp_bind(pcb, IP_ADDR_ANY, 123);
    udp_connect(pcb, ip, 123);
    struct pbuf *p = pbuf_alloc(PBUF_TRANSPORT, 48, PBUF_RAM);
    uint8_t *payload = (uint8_t *)p->payload;
    memset(payload, 0, 48);
    *payload = 0x1b;
    err_t er = udp_send(pcb, p);
    pbuf_free(p);
}
```

```c
struct timeStatus *getSNTP()
{
    struct timeStatus *tstatus = malloc(sizeof(struct timeStatus));
    tstatus->ready = false;
    tstatus->pcb=NULL;
    ip_addr_t ip;
    cyw43_arch_lwip_begin();
    err_t err = dns_gethostbyname("time.nist.gov",
                                        &ip, dns_found, tstatus);
    cyw43_arch_lwip_end();
    if (err == ERR_OK)
    {
        printf("DNS cache %s\n", ipaddr_ntoa(&ip));
        dns_found("", &ip, tstatus);
    }
    return tstatus;
}
void cancelSNTP(struct timeStatus *tstatus)
{
    if (tstatus != NULL)
    {
        udp_remove(tstatus->pcb);
        free(tstatus);
        tstatus = NULL;
        printf("canceled\n");
    }
}
int main()
{
    stdio_init_all();
    connect();
    while (true)
    {
        struct timeStatus *tstatus = getSNTP();
        sleep_ms(500);
        if (pollSNTP(tstatus))
            break;
        cancelSNTP(tstatus);
    }
    while (true)
    {
        struct tm t;
        getDateNow(&t);
        char Date[100];
        strftime(Date, sizeof(Date),
                    "Date: %a, %d %b %Y %k:%M:%S %Z\r\n", &t);
        printf("%s\n", Date);
        sleep_ms(5000);
    }
}
```

The `CmakeLists.txt` file has to include the `rtc` library:

```
target_link_libraries(main pico_stdlib
        pico_cyw43_arch_lwip_threadsafe_background
                hardware_rtc)
```

and the `lwipopts.h` file is unmodified.

A Better SNTP Client

The SNTP client that we have developed is very basic. It is suitable for setting the RTC clock at the start of an application, but it misses the ability to automatically refresh the time, use multiple time servers, take the round trip estimates in consideration to improve the accuracy and it doesn't check for a wide range of error conditions. All of this might be irrelevant to the application and trading sophistication for simplicity is often valid. However, if you do need something more robust then, rather than continuing to improve the very basic SNTP client, it is more sensible to make use of the SNTP app provided by lwIP. The only problem with this is that its documentation doesn't really help with getting started. The good news is that it is fairly easy.

The SNTP app has two operating modes, polling and listening. In polling mode it queries the SNTP server at a set interval. In listening mode it simply waits for the server to send a packet.

To set up the mode you have to use:

```
sntp_setoperatingmode(SNTP_OPMODE_POLL);
```

or `SNTP_OPMODE_LISTENONLY` .

You can get the operating mode using:

```
u8_t sntp_getoperatingmode (void)
```

You can set the polling time in the `lwiopts.h` file:

```
#define SNTP_UPDATE_DELAY       60*1000
```

sets the poll time to 60 seconds. Notice that you cannot set this value to less than 15 seconds as the SNTP standard doesn't allow it.

Next you have to set up the SNTP servers that you are using. A list of servers is maintained as an array. You can set the size of the array in `lwipopts.h`:

```
#define SNTP_MAX_SERVERS   1
```

The documentation only mentions being able to set servers by IP address:

```
void sntp_setserver (u8_t idx, const ip_addr_t *server)
const ip_addr_t *sntp_getserver (u8_t idx)
```

where idx is the index into the server array.

However, if you set:

```
#define SNTP_SERVER_DNS                 1
```

in lwipopts.h then you can also use:

```
void sntp_setservername(u8_t idx, const char *server)
const char *sntp_getservername(u8_t idx)
```

Finally, when you have all this set up you can start the client running using:

```
sntp_init();
```

and stop it using:

```
sntp_stop();
```

Putting all this together gives a simple program for configuring and running the SNTP client:

```
sntp_setoperatingmode(SNTP_OPMODE_POLL);
sntp_setservername(0, "pool.ntp.org");
sntp_init();
```

Now the SNTP client is getting the time from the configured time server every so often as set in lwipopts.h. The question is how can you make use of this? In our case the question is how to set the RTC?

The answer is that you have to define one of the many time set, and perhaps time get, macros. The simplest to use is SNTP_SET_SYSTEM_TIME_NTP which passes the timestamp as a 32-bit word for seconds and microseconds. You can put the definition in the sntp.c file, but it is better to place it in lwipopts.h along with other customizations:

```
#define SNTP_SET_SYSTEM_TIME_NTP(sec, us) \
  void SNTPSetRTC(u32_t, u32_t); \
  SNTPSetRTC(sec, us)
```

This declares and calls the function SNTPSetRTC whenever there is an update. Notice you can call the function whatever you like, but it has to accept the two parameters.

You can define the SNTPSetRTC function along with your main program and in this case it follows the pattern given in the previous example:

```
void SNTPSetRTC(u32_t t, u32_t us)
{
    printf("updating RTC\n");
    time_t seconds_since_1970 = t - 2208988800;
    struct tm *datetime = gmtime(&seconds_since_1970);
    datetime_t dt;
    dt.year = datetime->tm_year + 1900;
    dt.month = datetime->tm_mon + 1;
    dt.day = datetime->tm_mday;
    dt.dotw = datetime->tm_wday;
    dt.hour = datetime->tm_hour;
    dt.min = datetime->tm_min;
    dt.sec = datetime->tm_sec;
    rtc_init();
    rtc_set_datetime(&dt);
}
```

The complete program is:

```
#include <stdio.h>

#include "pico/stdlib.h"
#include "pico/cyw43_arch.h"
#include "setupWifi.h"
#include "hardware/rtc.h"
#include <time.h>
#include "lwip/apps/sntp.h"

void SNTPSetRTC(u32_t t, u32_t us)
{
    printf("updating RTC\n");
    time_t seconds_since_1970 = t - 2208988800;
    struct tm *datetime = gmtime(&seconds_since_1970);
    datetime_t dt;
    dt.year = datetime->tm_year + 1900;
    dt.month = datetime->tm_mon + 1;
    dt.day = datetime->tm_mday;
    dt.dotw = datetime->tm_wday;
    dt.hour = datetime->tm_hour;
    dt.min = datetime->tm_min;
    dt.sec = datetime->tm_sec;
    rtc_init();
    rtc_set_datetime(&dt);
}
```

```
bool getDateNow(struct tm *t)
{
    datetime_t rtc;
    bool state = rtc_get_datetime(&rtc);
    if (state)
    {
        t->tm_sec = rtc.sec;
        t->tm_min = rtc.min;
        t->tm_hour = rtc.hour;
        t->tm_mday = rtc.day;
        t->tm_mon = rtc.month - 1;
        t->tm_year = rtc.year - 1900;
        t->tm_wday = rtc.dotw;
        t->tm_yday = 0;
        t->tm_isdst = -1;
    }
    return state;
}

int main()
{
    stdio_init_all();
    connect();

    sntp_setoperatingmode(SNTP_OPMODE_POLL);
    sntp_setservername(0, "pool.ntp.org");
    sntp_init();

    while (true)
    {
        struct tm t;
        if (getDateNow(&t))            {
            char Date[100];
            strftime(Date, sizeof(Date),
                        "Date: %a, %d %b %Y %k:%M:%S %Z\r\n", &t);
            printf("%s\n", Date);
        }
        sleep_ms(5000);
    }
}
```

The main program simply prints the date and time every five seconds after checking that the RTC is running. The additions needed to the lwipopts.h file are:

```
#define SNTP_SERVER_DNS                 1
#define SNTP_SUPPORT                    1
#define SNTP_UPDATE_DELAY        60*1000
#define SNTP_SET_SYSTEM_TIME_NTP(sec, us) \
 void SNTPSetRTC(u32_t, u32_t); \
  SNTPSetRTC(sec, us)
```

The `CmakeLists.txt` file is the same as the previous example.

There are a great many configuration parameters that you can set to modify how the program works. These are listed in:

`pico-sdk/lib/lwip/src/include/lwip/apps/sntp_opts.h`

In most cases it is better not to change this configuration file, but to put your changes in `lwipopts.h`.

You can configure the client to use multiple SNTP servers, accept SNTP server settings from the DHCP server, monitor the reachability of each server and so on. Of course, there is nothing stopping you from using the increased resolution, beyond one second, to set other hardware to a more accurate time.

Summary

- SNTP is a simple UDP-based protocol for acquiring the UTC time and date.

- The basic transaction is to send a UDP packet to port 123 and then wait for the server to respond with a packet that contains timestamps.

- Each time packet consists of four 32-bit words of general information followed by four 64- bit timestamps.

- The timestamps consist of four bytes giving the seconds and four bytes giving the fractional seconds since the fiducial date, which is midnight on January 1, 1900.

- The time rollover in 2036 has be dealt with by adding a 64-bit era timestamp, which isn't transmitted along with the time data but is derived locally and added. This is, in essence, changing the fiducial date at each rollover.

- The four timestamps can be used to correct the received time to allow for network delays.

- The key timestamp is TTS, the last of the four, which gives the time at the server when the packet was sent. In many cases this is the only timestamp used.

- It is easy to set up an SNTP client as the request for a time update takes the form of a 48-byte buffer with its first byte set to 0x23. This has to be sent using UDP to port 123.

- The response is a 48-byte buffer and the time in seconds at the server is stored in bytes 40 to 44 in big endian format.

- The received timestamp can easily be converted to a Linux/Unix timestamp and used to set the RTC.

- The correct way to find a SNTP time server is to use DNS to query a time pool server. This has a list of actual time servers which it supplies in rotation to even out the load.

- A particular problem with using lwIP is that its DNS implementation always caches DNS lookups which means that a DNS lookup of the pool server always returns the same time server.

- The lwIP library also provides an SNTP server module which has many additional features. It is easy to use provided you know how to configure it and how to use it to access the time or set the RTC.

Chapter 9

SMTP For Email

Email is one of the simplest of protocols and potentially very useful, however, the need to deal with spam has added layers of protection that makes it very difficult to actually send an email using the standard mail transport Simple Mail Transport Protocol, SMTP. If you are planning to use email to send data back to a central server or to a user then you are going to have to find a suitable server that will accept the connection. This usually means setting up your own mail server or finding a hosted mail server that has suitable security settings.

SMTP Protocol

While SMTP originated as a simple protocol, it has become very complex due to the range of security measures that have been added to it over time.

All SMTP commands and responses are text commands. You can even connect to an SMTP server using Telnet and conduct the session manually by typing in commands and reading the replies.

The first command is always:

`HELO` *domain making the connection*

The server will respond with a greeting message and the SMTP transaction has started. Of course, if the domain you specify is blacklisted or has other suspicious characteristics the server will immediately terminate the connection. You can also use `EHLO`, the Extended HELO, for servers that implement more than just the basic SMTP commands.

Most servers will also respond with a list of optional commands that they support. For example:

```
250-PIPELINING
250-SIZE 15728640
250-ETRN
250-STARTTLS
250-ENHANCEDSTATUSCODES
250-8BITMIME
250-DSN
250 SMTPUTF8
```

Now we can send a batch of emails if we want to.

When SMTP first started you could deposit email into any SMTP server and expect it to be delivered to wherever it needed to go. That is, they would relay mail from any user to any user.

Unfortunately spammers started to use arbitrary SMTP servers to send lots of emails to users who didn't want them. As a result most SMTP servers will not relay emails to other SMTP servers and as a result most will only accept email to the domain that they serve, i.e. the one that the MX records correspond to. You cannot just drop an email into any old SMTP server and expect it to deliver it to another SMTP server – in the early days of the Internet you could.

You will notice that this restriction effectively breaks the whole email system. How can a user send an email to a location remote from their local SMTP server and expect it to be sent on to its destination? After all, the server is usually set up to only accept emails destined for the local users. The solution is that SMTP servers which are expected to deliver mail to the wider Internet allow local users to login with a user name and password and if this is successful they will send, or relay, email to other SMTP servers. The alternative is to open the SMTP server and allow anyone to use it to relay mail. This is called an "open relay" and it will cause the server to be added to blacklists everywhere.

The next command you need is:

`MAIL FROM:` *from address*

The *from address* is used as a return address and it might even be looked up to see if it is on a white/black list if the server is performing spam filtering. Again, if the server doesn't like the *from address* the connection is closed.

To specify who the email is to you have to use:

`RCPT TO:` *to address*

As already noted, this generally has to be an address hosted by the server unless the server has been set up to relay emails to other servers.

After this you can send the body of the email as a multi-line text packet with the end marked by a line starting with a dot and nothing else.

To close the session you use the

`QUIT`

command.

All of the commands are accepted by the server, processed and a response is sent back.

The response can be more than one line and this complicates things just a little. Each line, however, starts with a code that indicates the status of the process - 250 means everything is fine and the command has been acted upon.

SMTP Ports

The standard SMTP port is 25, but many ISPs block this port to stop users running mail servers. This is a reasonably well-known fact and it is some times misinterpreted as meaning that port 25 is no longer used. This isn't the case as it is used by SMTP servers to connect to other SMTP servers to transfer mail, but to understand what is going on we need to consider things a little more generally.

There are two distinct roles that an SMTP server can play: submission and relay. Submission is where an email is sent by an SMTP client to a server – it is where an email gets into the system. Once into the system the SMTP server relays it to another SMTP server to get it closer to the delivery address. In the early days of the Internet SMTP servers would relay multiple times, but today nearly all send the email to the SMTP server that hosts its address in one go.

Port 25 is universally used for relay and it is also usually set up for submission, but it isn't recommended for this purpose and it is usually blocked by ISPs providing Internet connections to end users.

Port 2525 is sometimes used in place of 25 as a way of getting round the blocking on port 25 by ISPs.

Port 587 is the port for encrypted submission using TLSstart.

Port 465 is the standard port for encrypted submissions using TLS.

We will examine the way that encryption is implemented later as most SMTP servers support it and many demand it.

What all of this means is that in most cases an IoT device operating in a home environment will have to connect to an SMTP server using either port 587 or port 465.

The SMTP Client App

The lwIP library has an SMTP app that makes it very easy to send an email using the standard email exchange protocol. SMTP uses TCP to make a reliable connection between two SMTP machines. One of the machines will play the role of the server and accept the connection and the other will play the role of a client and transfer mail to the server. Notice that SMTP provides no way for a client to download email intended for it. To do this you need to implement either POP or IMAP.

The SMTP client app adds a few simple functions. You first need to set the mail server's IP address and port:

```
smtp_set_server_addr("iopress.info");
smtp_set_server_port(25);
```

You can use an IP address or a URL to specify the mail server.

At this point you might want to submit a user name and password, but most servers working without encryption don't support this and you will generally find that you are limited to sending emails only to users directly supported on the server. That is, there is no option to use the server to relay emails to other SMTP servers. Where authorization is required use:

```
smtp_set_auth("username", "password");
```

If there is no username and password then set both to NULL.

Once everything has been set up we can send an email:

```
smtp_send_mail("from address", "to address", "subject",
                                        "body", mailsent, NULL);
```

The email is constructed from "subject" and "body" which are both in general character arrays. The mailsent function is a callback that is invoked when the email has been sent with the results.

Putting all this together gives us a simple main program to send an email:

```
#include <stdio.h>
#include "pico/stdlib.h"
#include "pico/cyw43_arch.h"
#include "setupWifi.h"

#include "lwip/apps/smtp.h"

void mailsent(void *arg, u8_t smtp_result, u16_t srv_err, err_t
err)
{
    printf("mail (%p) sent with results: 0x%02x, 0x%04x, 0x%08x\n",
arg,
            smtp_result, srv_err, err);
}

int main()
{
    stdio_init_all();
    connect();

    smtp_set_server_addr("iopress.info");
    smtp_set_server_port(25);
    smtp_set_auth(NULL, NULL);
    smtp_send_mail("person1@iopress.info",
        "person2@iopress.info", "subject", "body", mailsent, NULL);
    while (true)
    {
        sleep_ms(10);
    }
}
```

We need to include `smtp.h`. We also need to modify the `CmakeLists.txt` to include the line:

```
target_link_libraries(main pico_stdlib
        pico_cyw43_arch_lwip_threadsafe_background pico_lwip_smtp)
```

Notice that we need to include `pico_lwip_smtp` because this is not included in the general lwIP interface.

If you try running this example you will probably find that it doesn't work. The reason is nothing to do with the program and everything to do with the configuration of the server.

The server has to be set up to allow a user registered to the server for mail to send an email to another user of the same server. This is the most likely configuration and it is where you should start when testing out how a server is configured.

There is a second reason why it is likely not to work. The `HELO/EHLO` command sends:

```
EHLO [192.168.253.58]
```

which is the local IP address of the Pico. Of course, this is not a routable address and IoT devices generally don't have addresses on the public internet. What usually happens is that a NAT router, which makes the connection to the Internet, uses its public IP address to send the email to the SMTP server. That is, the SMTP server receives packets that are to port 25, but from the public address of the NAT router.

The router keeps track of NAT connections by using a specific return port for each machine it provides access to the Internet. So the SMTP server takes a packet from the public address of the router, to port 25 with a return port address of 3245, say. When the server receives a packet to its public address specifying port 3245, it then converts this into a packet to the local IP of the Pico and to whatever return port the Pico set, usually 25 in this case. This is how NAT provides internet connections to local machines. The problem is that the SMTP server now sees multiple IP addresses and no domain names. How the server reacts to this depends on how it is set up. Many will reject the connection simply because no domain name is used and the IP address supplied is dynamic and so not trustworthy.

For example, the Postfix SMTP server is very often configured to reject any connection that cannot provide a domain name in its `HELO/EHLO` command. If you have control of the server check in `helo_access.pcre` for the line:

```
/(\d{1,3}[\.-]\d{1,3}[\.-]\d{1,3}[\.-]\d{1,3})/
                        REJECT ACCESS DENIED
```

This indicates your email was rejected because the sending mail server appeared to be on a dynamic IP address that should not be doing direct mail delivery. If you want to accept such mail find the line in in `helo_access.pcre` and comment it out.

So many things can go wrong that you need to consult the SMTP server's log to see the reason why the connection has been rejected. It is also almost essential to add:

```
#define SMTP_DEBUG    LWIP_DBG_ON
```

to the `lwipopts.h` file. This ensures that you see most of the commands passed between the client and the server. However, you will still not always see the reasons why things fail.

In short, there is nothing wrong with this SMTP client, but finding an SMTP server that will accept it is difficult if you do not control the server.

TLS SMTP Client

As already mentioned, most SMTP servers do not allow remote users unless the connection is encrypted. Adding TLS encryption to our SMTP example is very easy as the client has been written using `altcp` and so we can simply use `altcp_tls` to convert it into an encrypted client. However, things are a little more complicated in getting it to work with a suitable server.

There are two ways that SMTP can be used with encryption. The first, and currently the most common, is to use the StartTLS command. The idea is that the server and client first make connection using plain text and then the client issues the StartTLS command to start a TLS handshake. After this is complete, assuming that the client and server can agree a cryptographic suite to use, then the rest of the session is conducted using a TLS encrypted connection. SMTP servers can be set up to use StartTLS on any port including port 25, but for submission the standard port is 587.

The second way of encrypting SMTP is to establish an encrypted TLS to TCP connection before starting the SMTP connection. This is conceptually simple, but there is no plain text preamble to establish that the port supports encryption. The standard submission port for this approach is 465. This was briefly deprecated in favor of port 587, but it was later reinstated. However, the impression that it should be avoided is still prevalent.

An additional problem is what do you call these two methods? You will encounter port 587 being called the "StartTLS submission port" or confusingly the "TLS submission port". By contrast port 465 is often called the "SMTPS port for SMTP over SSL" or the "SSL port", even though like port 587 it uses TLS. You will also encounter the StartTLS method referred to as "explicit TLS" and the alternative referred to as "implicit TLS".

What does all of this have to do with the SMTP client? The answer is that it only supports implicit TLS or SMTPS and this means it generally should connect on port 465. More importantly it doesn't work with ports that only support StartTLS.

As an example we can create an SMTP client which can send mail using Gmail's SMTP server. This is a commonly suggested SMTP server to use, but it has its problems. The documentation states:

Gmail SMTP server address: smtp.gmail.com
Gmail SMTP name: Your full name
Gmail SMTP username: Your full Gmail address (e.g. you@gmail.com)
Gmail SMTP password: The password that you use to log in to Gmail
Gmail SMTP port (TLS): 587
Gmail SMTP port (SSL): 465

This makes it look easy – all we have to do is connect using TLS to port 465 and supply the Gmail user name and password. Notice that this isn't really a good idea in an IoT device as the password would be easy to find. To make use of this in a production environment you would have to set up a special email account that the devices could use. Even then the fact that the password has to be in plain text in the program means that anyone with access to the IoT device could start using the same server account to send spam.

There is another problem that the documentation doesn't refer to. If an application is connecting to the service it needs its own password – an application password. To create one you have to go to the Google account, select security, and then under Signing in to Google, select App Passwords. From here you can use Select app to generate a Gmail password for your program. In other words, the fourth step in the documentation should read:

Gmail SMTP password: The password you generated for your app.

Now we can modify the previous program to make use of SMTP. This is a very small modification, but notice that we have to change CmakeLists and include a suitable mbedtls_config.h:

```
#include <stdio.h>

#include "pico/stdlib.h"
#include "pico/cyw43_arch.h"

#include "setupWifi.h"
#include "lwip/altcp_tls.h"
#include "lwip/apps/smtp.h"

void mailsent(void *arg, u8_t smtp_result,
                            u16_t srv_err, err_t err)
{
    printf("mail (%p) sent with results:
            0x%02x, 0x%04x, 0x%08x\n", arg,
                            smtp_result, srv_err, err);
}
```

```
int main()
{
    stdio_init_all();
    connect();
    struct altcp_tls_config *tls_config =
                        altcp_tls_create_config_client(NULL, 0);
    smtp_set_tls_config(tls_config);

    smtp_set_server_addr("smtp.gmail.com");
    smtp_set_server_port(465);
    smtp_set_auth("gmail address", "app password");

    smtp_send_mail("gmail address", "recipients address",
                        "subject", "body", mailsent, NULL);
    while (true)
    {
        sleep_ms(10);
    }
}
```

The only differences are the use of port 465, the need to specify the user name and app password and the addition of:

```
struct altcp_tls_config *tls_config =
                        altcp_tls_create_config_client(NULL, 0);
smtp_set_tls_config(tls_config);
```

Notice that with this configuration you can send an email to anyone, not just people using the same SMTP server. Also notice that the client doesn't need a certificate. You can use one if you want to but if so it has to be a properly issued certificate, not just a self-signed certificate.

The CmakeLists.txt file has to include the line:

```
target_link_libraries(main pico_stdlib
pico_cyw43_arch_lwip_threadsafe_background pico_lwip_mbedtls
pico_mbedtls pico_lwip_smtp)
```

and the lwipops.h file has to include:

```
#undef TCP_WND
#define TCP_WND                 16384
#undef MEM_SIZE
#define MEM_SIZE                8000

#define LWIP_ALTCP              1
#define LWIP_ALTCP_TLS          1
#define LWIP_ALTCP_TLS_MBEDTLS  1

#define LWIP_DEBUG 1
#define ALTCP_MBEDTLS_DEBUG     LWIP_DBG_ON
#define SMTP_DEBUG              LWIP_DBG_ON
```

You also need a suitable `mbedtls_config.h` and you can use almost any of the examples given previously as mail servers tend to support the same range of crypto suites as web servers – the one that worked with Google can be found on the book's page at www.iopress.info.

Working with IoT Email

Both of the example programs given in this chapter are correct and implement unencrypted and encrypted email respectively. However, as already mentioned, the fact that they are correct doesn't mean they will work with any particular server. Defenses against spam email are so strong and complicated that it is hard to avoid tripping them even if you aren't sending spam. To do the job properly you would need a domain name for the client to use and you would have to implement the modern mechanisms for avoiding spam – DKIM, DMARC, and SPF. Even then there is no certainty that a cautious server will not reject your email because you are on one of the many blacklists or because it just doesn't like the color of the bits you are sending.

The only way to be sure that you can deliver an email from an IoT device to an SMTP server is to run and configure the server yourself. This isn't easy due to the precautions needed to avoid it being used for spam while serving your IoT devices. It is difficult to lock down a server that has to allow IoT devices to connect. The reason is that while you can use encryption to protect the data, and the username and password in particular, any attacker that has physical access to the device can quickly find out what these are. To stop the server from being used to send spam you have to also restrict recipients to the server's domain, i.e. no relaying even for logged in users. This limits the usefulness of the server to the IoT devices it serves.

If you do have a use case where sending emails from an IoT device is useful then you also need to be aware of what is missing from the SMTP client application. You can use it to send text-based emails, but if you want to send binary data or "file" attachments then you will have to implement your own MIME support. Email clients in more complete libraries build emails that include multiple headers and MIME types. The only header that the SMTP client adds to your email is the subject line.

Overall using email in an IoT context seems like a reasonable idea at first, if only because email is universally supported and human readable. However, once you start to contend with the need to reduce spam and maintain security it becomes less attractive.

Summary

- SMTP is a simple protocol that has evolved to become very complex due to the need to add security.

- All SMTP commands are sent in human readable text and you can even talk to a server using telnet.

- After opening an SMTP connection the server will generally send a list of the features it supports.

- SMTP servers used to accept mail from anyone and deliver it to anyone, but the need to fight spam has changed this so that a server will accept outgoing email only from users on its local network or users that are authenticated and will only accept incoming mail addressed users on its local network.

- Port 25 used to be the only port used by SMTP, but today it is mainly used for connections between SMTP servers delivering mail. If you want to submit mail to an SMTP server then you might well find that port 25 is blocked to you.

- Port 587 is used for encrypted TLS connection mediated using TLSstart. It is also called the SMTPS port or just the SSL port.

- Port 465 is used for SMTP over a TLS connection which is set up before the SMTP transaction starts. Often called implicit TLS, it is used by lwIP and so you should connect using port 465.

- You can connect to the Gmail SMTP server on port 465, but you need to obtain a special password for your applications.

- Hard coding an SMTP password into your program is a big security risk.

- The big problem with using SMTP is that the majority of servers will reject your attempt to submit email without authentication.

So far we have been exploring protocols that haven't been invented specifically for the IoT, Internet of Things. A simple device can make use of HTTP to send data to a server or email, but neither of these have characteristics that make them suitable for IoT use unless you add additional processing to the server.

Consider the simple application of a sensor that reads the temperature and needs to make this available to other devices. You can use HTTP to send data to the server and save it in a file, but you will have to make sure that the data is saved in a suitable format to allow clients to process it. For example, you will need to make sure that it is dated and fed to clients in the correct order. An IoT-specific protocol would make tasks such as these much easier and MQTT – originally standing for Message Queue Telemetry Transport – is exactly this. It is lightweight, easy to use and popular so let's take a look at how to use the MQTT client included in lwIP.

Principles of MQTT

MQTT is a publish-and-subscribe messaging system. What this means is that there are clients which submit messages to a server, or broker, which sends them on to clients that are subscribed to the topic. Messages are organized by topics and clients can be subscribed to messages on multiple topics.

The connections between client and server are via TCP and optionally TLS-encrypted TCP. The data packets are binary-encoded and not human-readable and there is no standard for the payload data that they carry. There is a mechanism for specifying the format of the payload data in MQTT 5, but most servers and clients, including lwIP, use MQTT 3.1. The advantage of using binary data is that MQTT packets can be small. However, TCP is not good at working with small packets and so it is generally important to keep the TCP connection alive while the client and server exchange packets.

This all sounds useful, but there are some important subtleties that you need to be aware of before you can see the sorts of things that MQTT can be easily used for. The first important point is that a client has to be subscribed to a topic to receive any published data. If a client publishes data then the server sends it to all of the clients that are currently connected and subscribed to the topic. MQTT has no memory of clients that were subscribed and are now disconnected – it is a stateless protocol. After it has been sent to all of the active subscribed clients, the data is deleted from the server. Again, by default, MQTT has no memory of what happens. The exception is that the server can set a retain flag on a message which causes the server not to delete it after sending it to subscribed clients. If another client connects before another message is published then it is sent the retained message as soon as it has subscribed. Notice that the server keeps only one retained message per topic. This is intended to allow clients to receive the most up-to-date message immediately after they subscribe rather than having to wait for the next published message.

It is also possible to set up a default message, humorously called the last will and testament, which is delivered if the publisher of a topic goes offline unexpectedly.

The key ideas are:

- MQTT is mostly a memoryless and stateless protocol.
- Messages are published and subscribed to under topics.
- A published message is sent to all currently connected clients subscribed to the topic and then it is deleted unless set to be retained.
- A message that has no current subscribers is immediately deleted.
- Messages can be set to be retained to be sent to new subscribers but are still deleted when a new message arrives.
- A publisher can also set a default message to be sent if the server becomes unavailable.

What all this means is that MQTT is an intermediary between clients and other clients. It allows a client to acquire data from an IoT device without the IoT device having to take on the responsibility and overheads of being a server. MQTT doesn't do anything about data aggregation, i.e. it doesn't store a time series of sensor data. Also notice that there is no sense in which MQTT operates as a queue of messages. Each message is distributed to the subscribed clients in the order that it was submitted but the messages are not retained in a queue for new subscribers to examine.

There are many online services that make use of MQTT as a communications method and add to this storage and analysis features of the data that is published.

An MQTT Server

Before we can get started implementing an MQTT client we need to have access to an MQTT server. There are two ways of achieving this. The first is that you can host your own or you can use a cloud-hosted server.

If you decided to host your own server the problem is reliability and access. One of the important characteristics of an MQTT server is that it has to be available 24/7 for IoT devices to send data to and for subscribers to read data from. Usually this means using a custom server in the cloud to pass the problem to a third party. This makes using a cloud-provided MQTT server attractive. On the other hand, if you don't need 24/7 availability, then hosting MQTT on local hardware isn't difficult and it is the lowest cost option with maximum flexibility.

If you want to host your own MQTT server then the two programs most commonly used are Mosquitto and HiveMQ.

Mosquitto is open source and the project is hosted by Eclipse. It runs on Linux, Windows and Mac and it is very easy to install and configure. You can also make use of a sandbox public server to try out your MQTT client, but this isn't suitable for anything but limited experimentation.

HiveMQ is available as a trial version limited to 25 connections and not for production use. This isn't particularly attractive for testing purposes but HiveMQ cloud provides a free to use public server which is suitable for very low volume use. The down side is that there is no uptime guarantee and you are limited to 100 devices and 10 GB of traffic per month. The HiveMQ Cloud also insists on TLS encryption.

For simplicity the examples in this chapter make use of the Mosquitto sandbox at test.mosquitto.org. It provides a range of differently configured servers on different ports:

```
1883 : MQTT, unencrypted, unauthenticated
1884 : MQTT, unencrypted, authenticated
8883 : MQTT, encrypted, unauthenticated
8884 : MQTT, encrypted, client certificate required
8885 : MQTT, encrypted, authenticated
8886 : MQTT, encrypted, unauthenticated
8887 : MQTT, encrypted, server certificate deliberately expired
8080 : MQTT over WebSockets, unencrypted, unauthenticated
8081 : MQTT over WebSockets, encrypted, unauthenticated
8090 : MQTT over WebSockets, unencrypted, authenticated
8091 : MQTT over WebSockets, encrypted, authenticated
```

Even with encryption you need to keep in mind that your data is not private – this is a testing facility.

A Simple MQTT Client

In general, there are two sorts of MQTT clients – publishers and subscribers. The same client generally doesn't implement both for the same topic, but it is not difficult in practice. To make things as simple as possible we can start with a client that publishes a message to the server without using any encryption.

There are two main structs used by the MQTT client. The first, `mqtt_client_t` is used by the program to keep track of the state of the connection. In general you create this, but then allow the MQTT code to manage it:

```
mqtt_client_t *client = mqtt_client_new();
```

The second, `mqtt_connect_client_info_t`, is used by your program to define the connection:

```
struct mqtt_connect_client_info_t {
  const char *client_id;
  const char* client_user;
  const char* client_pass;
  u16_t keep_alive;
  const char* will_topic;
  const char* will_msg;
  u8_t will_qos;
  u8_t will_retain;
};
```

The `client_id` is the only field you have to use and it sets a unique identifier for the connection. It is common to use the MAC address of the client to ensure that it is unique. The `client_user` and `client_pass` are only used if a user name and password are required to connect. The `keep_alive` field specifies how many seconds before the client should "ping" the server. TCP connections are usually terminated after an idle timeout and to stop the MQTT client from being automatically disconnected you have to set `keep_alive` to a time that is shorter than the timeout. The remaining four fields are used to set the `will_msg` message that is sent to subscribers to the topic specified by `will_topic` if the publisher disconnects without closing the connection down.

There is a final field included if you are using TLS:

```
struct altcp_tls_config *tls_config;
```

which specifies the configuration of the TLS connection. This is explained more fully later.

You have to create an `mqtt_connect_client_info_t` struct and initialize it:

```
struct mqtt_connect_client_info_t ci;
```

Any fields that you are not using have to be zeroed so it is simpler to set the whole struct to zero before using it:

```
memset(&ci, 0, sizeof(ci));
```

The only field we need for a simple connection is the client's unique id and usually the keep_alive field:

```
ci.client_id = "MyPicoW";
ci.keep_alive = 10;
```

Now we are ready to make the connection. Usually you would use the DNS module to look up the URL of the MQTT server, but for this example we can use its IP address directly:

```
ip_addr_t ip;
IP4_ADDR(&ip, 137, 135, 83, 217);
```

This is the IP address of test.mosquitto.org at the time of writing – you need to check this before running the program or implement DNS lookup in the example.

To make the connection we need to pass the client, IP address, port number, a callback and the client info:

```
err_t err = mqtt_client_connect(client, &ip, 1883,
mqtt_connection_cb, 0, &ci);
```

The callback is called when the connection has been made. After this we can start to publish and subscribe to topics. To disconnect you use:

```
mqtt_disconnect(client);
```

The callback needs to check that the connection worked and in most cases set a status variable so that the program can start to use the connection:

```
void mqtt_connection_cb(mqtt_client_t *client, void *arg,
mqtt_connection_status_t status)
{
    if (status == MQTT_CONNECT_ACCEPTED)
    {
        mqttStatus = 1;
    }
}
```

Of course you could use arg to pass in the status rather than a global and it would be more flexible to use a struct, but a using a global makes for a simpler example.

Sending a Message

Now that we have a connection we can call the function that sends a message:

```
char payload[] = "Hello MQTT World";
u8_t qos = 2;
u8_t retain = 0;
err_t err = mqtt_publish(client, "MyTopic", payload,
            strlen(payload), qos, retain, pub_request_cb, client);
```

The second parameter sets the topic and the third is the payload. Notice that the payload is actually a void*, i.e. a pointer to anything, and so it can be anything including pure binary data. The qos parameter sets the quality of service which determines how often the subscriber will receive:

0   At most once
1   At least once
2   Exactly once

Obviously ensuring even a single delivery takes more resources. The retain parameter simply asks for the server to keep the message until the next message is received or to discard the message after the last delivery. The pub_request_cb callback is called when the message has been published:

```
static void pub_request_cb(void *arg, err_t result)
{
    printf("Publish result: %d\n", result);
    mqtt_client_t *client = (mqtt_client_t *)arg;
}
```

Subscribing to a Topic

Receiving a message that you have subscribed to is slightly more complicated. The function to subscribe is simple enough:

```
err_t err = mqtt_subscribe(client, "MyTopic", 1,
                                sub_request_cb, NULL);
```

The third parameter specifies the quality of service and the sub_request_cb callback is called when the subscription request has been processed. Ideally you need to set up two callbacks before you subscribe:

```
mqtt_set_inpub_callback(client, incoming_publish_cb,
                                incoming_data_cb, NULL);
```

The first, incoming_publish_cb, is called when a message is available. Notice that this is any message that you have subscribed to. The second is called after the first to deliver the payload. As MQTT messages can be large, the incoming_data_cb callback can be called more than once to build up a complete message.

The first callback is:

```
static void incoming_publish_cb(void *arg, const char *topic,
                                              u32_t tot_len)
{
    printf("Topic %s. %d\n", topic, tot_len);
}
```

You can use the topic parameter to decide what to do with the message that follows. The tot_len gives the total length of the message which may be sent split into smaller packets. The callback that processes the data is:

```
static void incoming_data_cb(void *arg, const u8_t *data,
                                       u16_t len, u8_t flags)
{
    char *payload = (char *)data;
    printf("payload\n%.*s\n", len, payload);
}
```

In this case because the message sent is so short we can be sure that just one packet is involved. In this case all we do is cast the u8_t data to char * and display it. Notice that data isn't a null-terminated string so we have to be careful how we process it. The printf will print a maximum of len characters. Notice that if data contains a zero byte the printing will stop there. In a more realistic application you would have to allow for the possibility that len did not equal totlen and multiple packets would need to be combined to get the final payload. The final parameter, flags, is equal to MQTT_DATA_FLAG_LAST when it is the last block of data.

The main Program

We can now put all this together to create a single program that connects to the MQTT server, sets up a subscription and then publishes data to it every few seconds. It is natural to use a polling loop approach and the status global variable:

```
#include <stdio.h>

#include "pico/stdlib.h"
#include "pico/cyw43_arch.h"
#include "lwip/ip_addr.h"
#include "setupWifi.h"
#include "lwip/altcp.h"
#include "lwip/apps/mqtt.h"
```

```c
int mqttStatus = 0;
int main()
{
 stdio_init_all();
 connect();
 mqtt_client_t *client = mqtt_client_new();

 struct mqtt_connect_client_info_t ci;
 memset(&ci, 0, sizeof(ci));
 ci.client_id = "MyPicoW";
 ci.keep_alive = 10;

    ip_addr_t ip;
    IP4_ADDR(&ip, 137, 135, 83, 217);

    err_t err = mqtt_client_connect(client, &ip,
                             1883, mqtt_connection_cb, 0, &ci);

    while (true)
    {
        switch (mqttStatus)
        {
            case 0:
            break;
            case 1:
                mqtt_set_inpub_callback(client,incoming_publish_cb,
                                    incoming_data_cb, NULL);
                err_t err = mqtt_subscribe(client, "MyTopic", 1,
                                        sub_request_cb, NULL);

                break;

            case 2:
                char payload[] = "Hello MQTT World";
                u8_t qos = 2;
                u8_t retain = 0;
                err_t err = mqtt_publish(client, "MyTopic", payload,
                    strlen(payload), qos, retain, pub_request_cb,
                                                        client);

                break;
        }
        sleep_ms(2000);
    }
}
```

The callbacks aren't listed, but they are as given earlier.

If you run this you will see:

```
Subscribe result: 0
Topic MyTopic. 16
payload
Hello MQTT World
Publish result: 0
Topic MyTopic. 16
payload
Hello MQTT World
Publish result: 0
 . . .
```

repeated every two seconds.

To make this work you need to change the `Cmakelists.txt` read:

```
target_link_libraries(main pico_stdlib
            pico_cyw43_arch_lwip_threadsafe_background
                                        pico_lwip_mqtt)
```

and the end of the `lwipopts.h` file read:

```
#define LWIP_ALTCP              1
#define MEMP_NUM_SYS_TIMEOUT    (LWIP_NUM_SYS_TIMEOUT_INTERNAL + 1)
#define MQTT_REQ_MAX_IN_FLIGHT  (5)
```

The number of available timers has to be increased as the MQTT client makes use of an extra one to time the keep alive feature. If you are having problems you might need to add:

```
#define MQTT_DEBUG              LWIP_DBG_ON
```

although the debug information isn't as useful as in the previous case of SMTP.

A complete listing can be found on the book's page at www.iopress.info.

MQTT TLS

Adding TLS security to the MQTT client is very easy but there is an interesting problem you might encounter if you use a server cluster like HiveMQ.

All you have to do is create a `altcp_tls_config` struct either with or without a certificate:

```
struct altcp_tls_config *tls_config =
altcp_tls_create_config_client(NULL, 0);
```

In this case no certificate is specified. If you do specify a certificate then the MQTT server generally has to be configured to make use of it. To tell the MQTT client to make use of it you have to set the appropriate field in the client info struct:

```
ci.tls_config = tls_config;
```

Of course to make this work you need to add:

```
#include "lwip/altcp_tls.h"
```

You also need to add to the lwipopts.h file:

```
#define LWIP_ALTCP_TLS          1
#define LWIP_ALTCP_TLS_MBEDTLS  1
```

and to the CmakeLists.txt file:

```
target_link_libraries(main pico_stdlib
pico_cyw43_arch_lwip_threadsafe_background pico_lwip_mqtt
pico_lwip_mbedtls
pico_mbedtls)
```

Now if you run the program so that it will connect to an MQTT port that accepts TLS connections, i.e. 8883 for the sandbox. Everything will work as before, but now all data transfer will be encrypted. The complete listing of the TLS version can be found on the book's webpage.

HiveMQ and the Server Name Problem

As an alternative to the Eclipse Mosquitto sandbox you can use HiveMQ which provides a server which is capable of being used to test and even run small configurations. The only problem is that a HiveMQ cluster runs a set of MQTT servers at the same address. This is just like the situation where a single HTTPS server supports multiple websites and the solution is the same, Server Name Indication. The only problem is that the MQTT client doesn't provide the opportunity of setting SNI even though it is available.

If you need to use SNI with TLS connection then there is no choice but to modify MQTT. The simplest way is to include a new field in the client info:

```
  u8_t will_retain;
  #if LWIP_ALTCP && LWIP_ALTCP_TLS
    /** TLS configuration for secure connections */
    struct altcp_tls_config *tls_config;
    char domName[100];
  #endif
};
```

The modification starts at line 85 in mqtt.h. The idea is that you set domName and the TLS connection will automatically add it if it is non-null:

```
#if LWIP_ALTCP && LWIP_ALTCP_TLS
  if (client_info->tls_config) {
    client->conn = altcp_tls_new(client_info->tls_config,
                                      IP_GET_TYPE(ip_addr));

    if(client_info->domname)
      mbedtls_ssl_set_hostname(altcp_tls_context(client→conn),
                                      client_info->domname);

  } else
#endif
```

This change starts at line 1382 in mqtt.c and the final else is not a mistake.

With this modification we can now change the main program of the previous example so that it makes use of HiveMQ with TLS, SNI and username/password authentication:

```c
int main()
{
    stdio_init_all();
    connect();
    struct altcp_tls_config *tls_config =
                        altcp_tls_create_config_client(NULL, 0);
    mqtt_client_t *client = mqtt_client_new();
    struct mqtt_connect_client_info_t ci;
    memset(&ci, 0, sizeof(ci));
    ci.client_id = "MyPicoW";
    ci.client_user = "username";
    ci.client_pass = "password";
    ci.keep_alive = 10;
    ci.tls_config = tls_config;
    strncpy(ci.domName,
     "1a6d2dccd35744888e4b7c6f8e65f613.s2.eu.hivemq.cloud", 100);
    ip_addr_t ip;
    IP4_ADDR(&ip, 20, 79, 70, 109);
    err_t err = mqtt_client_connect(client, &ip, 8883,
                                    mqtt_connection_cb, 0, &ci);
    char payload[] = "Hello MQTT World";
    u8_t qos = 2;
    u8_t retain = 0;
    while (true)
    {
        switch (mqttStatus)
        {
         case 0:
            break;
         case 1:
            mqtt_set_inpub_callback(client, incoming_publish_cb,
                                    incoming_data_cb, NULL);
            err = mqtt_subscribe(client, "MyTopic", 1,
                                    sub_request_cb, NULL);
            break;
         case 2:
            err = mqtt_publish(client, "MyTopic", payload,
             strlen(payload), qos, retain, pub_request_cb, client);
            break;
        }
        sleep_ms(2000);
    }
}
```

The callbacks and all of the other files stay the same. A complete listing can be found on the book's webpage at www.iopress.info.

Summary

- MQTT makes use of a central server to allow clients to exchange messages.

- Publishers connect to the server and send messages labelled by topic. The server sends each message to all of the clients subscribed to the topic and then, by default, deletes the message.

- Clients do not see messages that occur while they are offline, but publishers can set a message to be retained until the next message is sent. Clients that connect to the server see the latest retained message.

- A publisher can also set a default message to be sent if the server becomes unavailable.

- Many online MQTT services add data aggregation, analysis and presentation but these are not part of MQTT.

- There are a number of MQTT servers, but two of the best known are the open source Mosquitto and the commercial HiveMQ. Both provide free to use services that are suitable for testing and low volume use.

- MQTT communications can be via TCP or TLS encrypted TCP implemented using altcp.

- Some MQTT servers, HiveMQ for example, share a single machine and these need Server Name Indication to determine which server is being addressed. This is not supported by altcp, but can easily be added.

Appendix 1

Getting Started In C

You have to use another computer system to develop programs for the Pico and at the moment three types of system are supported – Linux, Windows and Mac OS. The Pico website has a definite preference for using Linux in the form of Pi OS running on a Pi 4 or a Pi 400. This is a very attractive option, but using Windows or a Mac may be preferable to any programmer familiar with their operating systems and ways of working.

You also have a choice of exactly how to create programs to run on the Pico – the editor or IDE to use. While the website attempts to be neutral and suggests that you can use almost anything, there are big advantages in opting to use Visual Studio Code, VS Code. It is a free, open source, multi-language editor that offers many features that make programming easier, faster and less error-prone. You would be well advised to adopt VS Code, even though it might take more time to get started if you haven't used it before. It is a general skill that will continue to be useful if and when you move away from programming the Pico in C.

Pico on Pi

Using a Pi 4, or a Pi 400 with its built-in keyboard, as the development machine is the recommended option. If you want to make Pico development as easy as possible, this is the way to go as there is an official installation script that does all of the work for you. All you have to do is download it from the Raspberry Pi site, set it to be executable and execute it:

```
wget https://raw.githubusercontent.com/
                         raspberrypi/pico-setup/master/pico_setup.sh
chmod +x pico_setup.sh
./pico_setup.sh
```

This works well and doesn't install anything you already have installed. You do have to reboot for it all to take effect, however.

The script does all of the steps that you could do for yourself:

1. Creates a `pico` directory in the user's home directory.
2. Installs the GCC ARM compiler, CMake and a support library:
   ```
   sudo apt install cmake gcc-arm-none-eabi
                            libnewlib-arm-none-eabi
   ```
3. Clones the GitHub SDK repository:
   ```
   git clone -b master https://github.com/raspberrypi/pico-
   sdk.git
   cd pico-sdk
   git submodule update --init
   cd ..
   ```
4. Clones the examples and playground repositories – these aren't essential:
   ```
   git clone -b master https://github.com/raspberrypi/
                                pico-examples.git
   ```
5. Sets up paths by defining `PICO_SDK_PATH`, `PICO_EXAMPLES_PATH`, `PICO_EXTRAS_PATH`, and `PICO_PLAYGROUND_PATH` in your `~/.bashrc`
6. Builds the `blink` and `hello_world` examples in
   `pico-examples/build/blink` and
   `pico-examples/build/hello_world`
7. Downloads and builds `picotool` and copies it to `/usr/local/bin` - this isn't essential.
8. Downloads and builds `picoprobe` - this is necessary to do easy debugging with another Pico acting as a SWD (Serial Wire Debug) device.
9. Downloads and compiles the debugging tool OpenOCD.
10. Downloads and installs Visual Studio Code.
11. Installs the required Visual Studio Code extensions.
12. Configures the Raspberry Pi UART for use with the Pico.

Notice that the only things you actually need installed to get started are the GCC ARM compiler, CMake and the SDK. The other items will be useful later.

Pico on Windows

As of SDK 1.5 there is an official installation script for Windows and it makes the job of getting started much simpler. You can find it at:

`https://github.com/raspberrypi/pico-setup-windows`

It is easy to use and it works.

To find the .exe file you first need to navigate to the latest releases:

Then download the appropriate installer from the Assets section.

And run the .exe file from the command prompt.

At the time of writing it automatically installs and configures the following:

1. Arm GNU Toolchain

2. CMake

3. Ninja

4. Python 3.9

5. Git for Windows

6. Visual Studio Code

7. OpenOCD

The installation provides a specially configured version of VS Code – Pico-Visual Studio Code and a Pico-configured PowerShell and Command Prompt. In fact the PowerShell is used to start VS Code with the correct environment parameters. It also installs Ninja as the make utility not the default Nmake.

You need to always ensure that you start VS Code using the Pico shortcut otherwise you will get an unconfigured VS Code that will not know how to compile your program.

Building a Program

First open VS Code – under PiOS it is in the Programming section of the menu and under Windows you need to use `Pico-Visual Studio Code` in the start menu. If you have installed everything using the installation script, it will be set up and ready to work with a CMake project.

That is, both the CMake and debug extensions will already be installed in VSCode and this is worth checking before moving on.

To build a program open the folder that the C `main` program is stored in. If the program has header files which refer to the SDK, VS Code will most likely regard them as errors – ignore these errors until you have built the program. The Pico makes use of the CMake build system. This takes a specification for the project and then outputs instructions to a lower-level build utility to actually create the executable program. The instructions that

CMake uses are usually stored in a file called CMakeLists.txt which is stored in the root of the project directory. In this case we only need a simple set of instructions that describes the project and makes clear that it uses the SDK.

Create a file called CMakeLists.txt in the project folder and enter:

```
cmake_minimum_required(VERSION 3.13)
set(PICO_BOARD pico_w)
set(CMAKE_C_STANDARD 11)
set(CMAKE_CXX_STANDARD 17)

include(pico_sdk_import.cmake)
project(main C CXX ASM)

pico_sdk_init()
add_executable(main
 main.c
)
target_include_directories(main
                          PRIVATE ${CMAKE_CURRENT_LIST_DIR})
target_link_libraries(main pico_cyw43_arch_none pico_stdlib)
pico_add_extra_outputs(main)
```

This states that the minimum version of CMake that this works with is 3.13. It then includes the file pico_sdk_import.cmake – this is a CMake file that defines how the entire SDK is to be built. You need this in nearly all of the projects you create.

If you are using a Pico W then you need to set PICO_BOARD to pico_w. In general this has to be set to the board you are actually using.

As we "include" pico_sdk_import.cmake this has to be copied into the root of the project. You can copy it from any existing project, but you can get an up-to-date copy from pico/pico-sdk/external.

The project statement defines the project to be one that uses C, C++ and ARM assembly – your main program might be in C but the rest of the project uses more. After that we indicate the standards in use and then make a call to a routine defined in pico_sdk_import.cmake which initializes the SDK part of the project.

The line:

```
target_link_libraries(blinky pico_cyw43_arch_none pico_stdlib)
```

lists the Pico SDK modules that we are using – in this case the WiFi library and the stdlib. The WiFi library generally needs to be configured and this means that you need to copy:

```
 pico-examples/pico_w lwipopts_examples_common.h
```

to the project directory and rename it lwipopts.h.

We also need to copy `pico_sdk_import.cmake` into the root of the project. You can get it from any existing project, but you can get an up-to-date copy from `pico/pico-sdk/external`.

The final stage is to get VS Code to use the CMake extension to first configure and then build the project. The extension often autodetects that you are working with a C program. If this doesn't work and the `CMakeLists.txt` file isn't detected then use the Command Palette to issue the command:

CMake Show Configure Command

The one very important aspect of configuring the system is defining which "Kit" to use. Essentially a kit is a compiler collection that can be used to build the project. As you have installed GCC you should see it in the list – if you don't see it then use the [Scan for kits] option. If you still don't see it check that it is installed and on the path. The GCC version that you need is GCC for arm-none-eabi which targets a "bare metal" machine like the Pico. This is at version 10.3.1 under Windows and 8.31 under Pi OS at the time of writing.

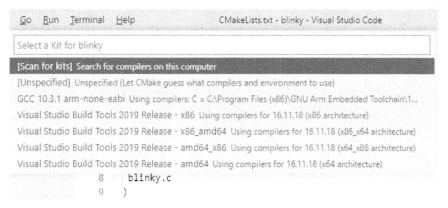

Don't select any kit which is called something like arm-linux-gnueabihf as these are versions of GCC which target Linux, i.e. they are what you would use to create a program to run on the Pi, not the Pico.

There are many ways to start a build of the project, but all of the commands are available if you select the CMake extension (by clicking on the icon at the left of the screen, the rectangle with a triangle in it) and then click on the three dots menu. The Clean Rebuild All Projects option rebuilds everything in the project including the SDK and files that haven't changed since the last build. A standard build only compiles files that have changed since the last compile.

For a first compile you will see a lot of messages about what is being compiled and so on and it will take a few minutes. On a subsequent build only files that have changed are recompiled and so things are quicker. Once the compile is complete you will find the results in the `build` directory. The file that you want in this instance is `main.uf2` which can be run by dragging-and-dropping it onto the USB drive that a connected Pico presents to the development machine.

Notice that if you have any problems or move the folder to a new location you can always delete the build directory and start again.

Checklist

If VS Code cannot complete a build and you have used the auto-installation scripts, then you need to check the following:

1. Have you created a `CmakeList.txt` file as well as `main.c`?

2. Have you copied `pico_sdk_import.cmake` from `pico/pico-sdk/external` into the project's directory? If you are using a Pico W you also need copy `pico-examples/pico_w lwipopts_examples_common.h`, to the project directory and rename it `lwipopts.h`.

3. Make sure that the selected kit is a version of `arm-none-eabi` which targets bare-metal machines like the Pico.

4. Try deleting the entire `build` directory and perform a clean rebuild.

5. If it still doesn't work, restart VS Code and try a clean configure and a clean rebuild.

Debugging Programs

To run the program, the simplest thing to do is connect a Pico to the development machine via USB. The USB connection will also power the Pico, and to get the Pico to present a USB drive to the development machine you have to hold down the BootSel button which is to the left of the USB connector as the power is applied.

If you have done this correctly you will see a new drive added to the development machine and you will have to supply a password to mount it:

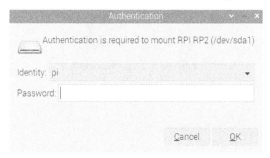

If you don't see this dialog box then you haven't held down the BootSel button while the power is being applied.

While this approach to running programs works for a first program, it isn't a sustainable way to develop programs for the Pico. You need to set up a debugger and how to do this depends on the machine you are using to create programs.

If you are using a Pi 4 or Pi 400 then it can be used as a debugging computer and all we need to do is add some connections to the Pico. If you are using any other machine the simplest solution is to use another Pico, which doesn't need WiFi, as a debugging computer and connect the debugging Pico to the development computer via USB.

Download and Debug Using a Pi 4

Debugging a Pico program when you are using a Pi 4 is particularly easy as it can do the job of the debugger. SWD, Serial Wire Debug, is a standard protocol for downloading programs and for debugging them on devices based on the Cortex M processor, such as the Pico.

The Pico has a debug connector at the bottom edge composed of three pins:

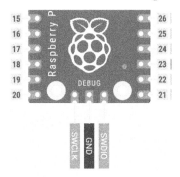

The connector on the Pico W is set back behind the WiFi unit:

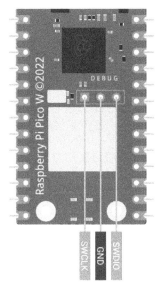

In both cases this is a three-wire interface consisting of ground, clock and data lines. These have to be connected either to another SWD three-wire interface or to three general purpose GPIO lines that have been programmed to work as an SWD interface. If you are using a Pi 4/400 to program the Pico

216

then three GPIO lines is the simpler option. By default the pins used are GND, GPIO24 and GPIO25:

Pi 4	Pi Pico
GPIO24 (Pin 18)	SWDIO
GND (Pin 20)	SWD GND
GPIO25 (Pin 22)	SWCLK

We also need to make a connection to the Pi 4 to host a serial connection so that the output of any `printf` commands has somewhere to be displayed. The Pico has a default UART connected to Pin 1 GP0 TX and Pin 2 GP1 RX. You simply need to connect the RX/TX pins to the corresponding TX/RX pins on the host machine.

Raspberry Pi	Raspberry Pi Pico
GND (Pin 14)	GND (Pin 3)
GPIO15 (UART_RX0, Pin 10)	GP0 (UART0_TX, Pin 1)
GPIO14 (UART_TX0, Pin 8)	GP1 (UART0_RX, Pin 2)

If you have already connected the Pico and the Pi together via the SWD interface you don't need to connect the GND as there is already a ground connection. If you are only interested in transmitting data from the Pico, you only need to connect Pin 1 and Pin 2.

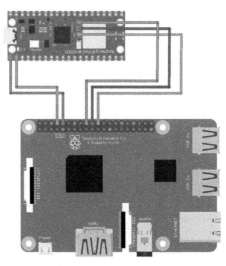

The hardware setup is simple, but you also need to use the:

```
sudo raspi-config
```

to set up the serial port on the Pi. Select Interfaces and then disable the Linux shell and enable the serial port. The system will reboot. After this you can use `serial0` to communicate with devices connected to the serial port.

To make the connection use:

```
sudo minicom -b 115200  -D /dev/serial0
```

Notice that you can do this in a terminal window in VS Code, which is the best way to work.

You also need to supply the Pico with a USB power connection, but this USB connection isn't used to download your program.

The most sensible thing to do is to move to VS Code, which makes running a program automatic and provides easy debug facilities. All you have to do is create a file called `launch.json` in the `.vscode` folder. Select the Cortex debugger if you are given a choice and change the generated file to read:

```
{
  "version": "0.2.0",
  "configurations": [
    {
      "name": "Cortex Debug",
      "cwd": "${workspaceRoot}",
      "executable": "${command:cmake.launchTargetPath}",
      "request": "launch",
      "type": "cortex-debug",
      "servertype": "openocd",
      "gdbPath": "gdb-multiarch",
      "device": "RP2040",
      "configFiles": [
        "interface/raspberrypi-swd.cfg",
        "target/rp2040.cfg"
        ],
      "svdFile":
      "${env:PICO_SDK_PATH}/src/rp2040/hardware_regs/rp2040.svd",
      "runToEntryPoint":"main",
      // Give restart the same functionality as runToMain
      "postRestartCommands": [
          "break main",
          "continue"
      ]
    }
  ]
}
```

Next you can select the debug configuration. Select the small green arrow labeled RUN in the Debug toolbar on the left. Select Pico Debug from the drop-down list and your program should be downloaded and run:

Although your program is running you won't see much happening because by default it is paused at the first instruction. You will see the debug toolbar appear and this is what you need to use to debug your program:

```
ninal  Help

C blinky.c    ::  ▶  ⤺  ⤓  ↑  ↻  ☐  ajson

C blinky.c > ⊕ main()
  1    #include "pico/stdlib.h"
  2
  3    int main() {
  4        const uint LED_PIN = 25;
  5        gpio_init(LED_PIN);
  6        gpio_set_dir(LED_PIN, GPIO_OU
```

To get the program running, simply click the blue triangle Run icon. You can also use the red square Stop icon to stop the program and the green circular arrow Restart icon to restart the program. If there are breakpoints in the code, click in the left-hand margin, the program will automatically stop and display the current state of variables in the left-hand debug pane. You can also single-step, step into called functions and step out of any called function. All of these also show you the current status of the variables. Notice that you have to stop the program using the Stop icon before you can rebuild it and run it again.

You now have a workable system that allows you to edit, build and debug Pico programs. You will need to modify the CMakeLists.txt file to include specific parts of the library as you make use of them, but this is fairly standard.

Debug Using PicoProbe

A Pi 4/400 can act as a host for VS Code, the SWD debugger and a serial connection for `printf`. This is because the Pi 4 has GPIO lines that can be used for the SWD connection and the serial interface while Windows and Linux computers generally don't have GPIO lines.

For other computers, Windows machines in particular, you need to use a SWD debugger to connect the Pico. One solution is to buy a SWD programmer, but it is easier, and usually cheaper, to use a second Pico to act as one.

You can make a general Pico into an SWD debugger with the help of a program called PicoProbe. You can also buy a dedicated Pico packaged ready to use as a debugger with PicoProbe installed and the correct sockets provided, making connection easier.

The connections to the second Pico, or to a PicoProbe, are:

PicoProbe	Pi Pico
GND	SWD GND
GP3	SWDIO
GP2	SWCLK

These are the only connections you need to make to turn the Pico into a SWD programmer. It is also a good idea to connect the Pico's serial pins, Pin 1 TX and Pin 2 RX to the PicoProbe's Pin 7 RX and Pin 6 TX respectively to implement a serial connection. The PicoProbe will present as a USB serial port to a Windows machine and there is no good reason not to use a Pico as the PicoProbe device.

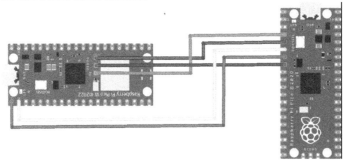

Both Picos need to be powered. The Pico that is running the program can be powered by a USB connection or any method you care to use. The PicoProbe, however, has to have a USB connection to the PC as this is the method used to communicate with it.

To make the Pico act like an SWD programmer you have to download the picoprobe program. You can find this on GitHub:

https://github.com/raspberrypi/picoprobe

or if you used the installation script, you will find a UF2 file, picoprobe.uf2, in pico/picoprobe/build. To install it all you have to do is connect power to the Pico while holding down the BootSel button and then drag-and-drop the UF2 file onto the USB driver that is installed on the PC. After this your Pico is a PicoProbe device whenever you turn it on.

If the two Picos are connected, powered and the PicoProbe is connected via USB to the PC or any other machine, we can start to use VS Code to run and debug new programs. All you have to do is create a file called launch.json in the .vscode folder containing:

```
{
    "version": "0.2.0",
    "configurations": [
    {
        "name": "Pico Debug",
        "cwd": "${workspaceRoot}",
        "executable": "${command:cmake.launchTargetPath}",
        "request": "launch",
        "type": "cortex-debug",
        "servertype": "openocd",
        "gdbPath": "arm-none-eabi-gdb",
        "device": "RP2040",
        "configFiles": [
        "interface/picoprobe.cfg",
        "target/rp2040.cfg"
         ],
        "svdFile":"${env:PICO_SDK_PATH}/src/rp2040/
                                   hardware_regs/rp2040.svd",
        "runToEntryPoint":"main",
   // Work around for stopping at main on restart
        "postRestartCommands": [
        "break main",
        "continue"
        ]
    }
  ]
}
```

Next you can select the debug configuration. Select the small green arrow labeled RUN in the Debug toolbar on the left. Select Pico Debug from the drop-down list and your program should be downloaded and run. You can use the debugger to single step and set breakpoints and if you connect to the serial port that corresponds to the USB serial port you will be able to see any output from the Pico.

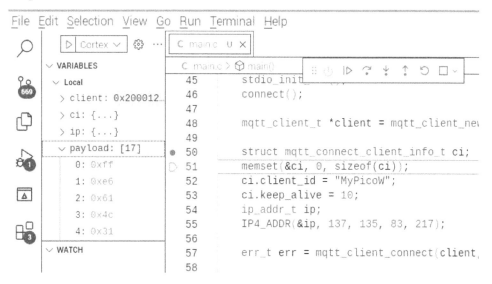

Index

228

Programming The Raspberry Pi Pico/W In C, Second Edition

ISBN: 978-1871962796

This introductory level book reveals what you can do with the Pico's GPIO lines together with widely used sensors, servos and motors and ADCs. It uses VS Code as the development environment and shows how to use a Raspberry Pi or a desktop PC running Windows as your development machine.

After covering the GPIO, outputs and inputs, events and interrupts, Harry gives you hands-on experience of PWM (Pulse Width Modulation), the SPI bus, the I2C bus and the 1-Wire bus. One of the key advantages of the Pico is its PIO (Programmable I/O) and while this is an advanced feature it is introduced in this book.

When the Raspberry Pi Pico was first introduced it lacked network connectivity. The Pico W remedied this shortcoming hence this second edition with additional material on its basic WiFi capabilities.

Programming The Raspberry Pi Pico/W In MicroPython, Second Edition

ISBN: 978-1871962802

This book combines Harry Fairhead's expertise in electronics and the IoT with Mike James' knowledge of Python. While you would choose C as the language for programming the Pico for maximum speed, MicroPython is a good alternative that it is easy to use. As a high-level language, MicroPython is based on Python 3 and is fully object-oriented. This means that you can create classes to encapsulate hardware and make it easier to use and understand.

The purpose of the book is to reveal what you can do with the Pico's GPIO lines together with widely used sensors, servos and motors and ADCs. After covering the GPIO, outputs and inputs, events and interrupts, it gives you hands-on experience of PWM (Pulse Width Modulation), the SPI bus, the I2C bus and the 1-Wire bus. One of the key advantages of the Pico is its PIO (Programmable I/O) and while this is an advanced feature, it is introduced in this book. After finding out how the PIO works, we apply it to writing a PIO program for the DHT22 and the 1-Wire bus. Two new chapters are dedicated to how to make use of the additional features of the Pico W including how to create a web client and a web server, use HTTPS and asyncio.

Raspberry Pi IoT in C, Second Edition
ISBN: 978-1871962635

This book takes a practical approach to understanding electronic circuits and datasheets and translating this to code, specifically using the C programming language. The main idea in this book is to not simply install a driver, but to work directly with the hardware using the Raspberry Pi's GPIO (General Purpose Input Output) to connect with off-the-shelf sensors.

Applying C For The IoT With Linux
ISBN: 978-1871962611

This book brings together low-level, hardware-oriented and often hardware-specific information. It starts by looking at how programs work with user-mode Linux. It explains the way Linux does things – pseudo file systems, threads, locking, arithmetic, files, atomics, sockets, memory mapping, low level graphics and more...

Fundamental C: Getting Closer To The Machine
ISBN: 978-1871962604

At an introductory level, this book explores C from the point of view of the low-level programmer. It covers addresses, pointers, and how things are represented using binary and emphasizes the important idea is that everything is a bit pattern and what it means can change.

When programming in C you need to think about the way data is represented, and this book emphasizes the idea of modifying how a bit pattern is treated using type punning and unions and tackles the topic of undefined behavior, which is ignored in many books on C. A particular feature of the book is the way C code is illustrated by the assembly language it generates. This helps you understand why C is the way it is. And the way it was always intended to be written - close to the metal.

Raspberry Pi IoT in Python With GPIO Zero
ISBN:9781871962666

Python is an excellent language to learn about the IoT or physical computing. It might not be as fast as C, but it is much easier to use for complex data processing. The GPIO Zero library is the official way to use Python with the GPIO and other devices. This book looks at how to use it to interface the Raspberry Pi 4 and Raspberry Pi Zero to IoT devices and at how it works so that you can extend it to custom devices. Studying GPIO Zero is also a great way to improve your Python.

Raspberry Pi IoT in C With Linux Drivers
ISBN:9781871962642

There are Linux drivers for many off-the-shelf IoT devices and they provide a very easy-to-use, high-level way of working. The big problem is that there is very little documentation to help you get started. This book explains the principles so that you can tackle new devices and provides examples of using external hardware via standard Linux drivers with the Raspberry Pi 4 and Raspberry Pi Zero in the C language, which provides optimal performance.

Raspberry Pi IoT in Python With Linux Drivers
ISBN:9781871962659

If you opt to use Linux drivers to connect to external devices then Python becomes a good choice, as speed of execution is no longer a big issue. This book explains how to use Python to connect to and control external devices with the Raspberry Pi 4 and Raspberry Pi Zero using the standard Linux drivers.

Programmer's Python: Everything is an Object, Second Edition
ISBN: 978-1871962741

This is the first in the *Something Completely Different* series of books that look at what makes Python special and sets it apart from other programming languages. It explains the deeper logic in the approach that Python 3 takes to classes and objects. The subject is roughly speaking everything to do with the way Python implements objects - metaclass; class; object; attribute; and all of the other facilities such as functions, methods and the many "magic methods" that Python uses to make it all work.

Programmer's Python: Everything is Data
ISBN: 978-1871962595

Following the same philosophy, this book shows how Python treats data in a distinctly Pythonic way. Python's data objects are both very usable and very extensible. From the unlimited precision integers, referred to as bignums, through the choice of a list to play the role of the array, to the availability of the dictionary as a built-in data type. This book is what you need to help you make the most of these special features.

Programmer's Python: Async
ISBN: 978-1871962595

An application that doesn't make use of async code is wasting a huge amount of the machine's potential. Subtitled "Threads, processes, asyncio & more", this volume is about asynchronous programming, something that is is hard to get right, but well worth the trouble and reveals how Python tackles the problems in its own unique way.

www.ingramcontent.com/pod-product-compliance
Lightning Source LLC
LaVergne TN
LVHW062314060326
832902LV00013B/2204